200 Best

Smoothie
Bowl Recipes

200 Best
Smoothie
Bowl Recipes

Alison Lewis

Robert
ROSE

200 Best Smoothie Bowl Recipes
Text copyright © 2016 Alison Lewis
Recipe photographs copyright © 2016 Robert Rose Inc.
Cover and text design copyright © 2016 Robert Rose Inc.

For complete cataloguing information, see page 232.

Disclaimer

The recipes in this book have been carefully tested by our kitchen and our tasters. To the best of our
knowledge, they are safe and nutritious for ordinary use and users. For those people with food or other
allergies, or who have special food requirements or health issues, please read the suggested contents of
each recipe carefully and determine whether or not they may create a problem for you. All recipes are
used at the risk of the consumer.

We cannot be responsible for any hazards, loss or damage that may occur as a result of any recipe use.

For those with special needs, allergies, requirements or health problems, in the event of any doubt,
please contact your medical adviser prior to the use of any recipe.

Design and production: Kevin Cockburn/PageWave Graphics Inc.
Editor: Sue Sumeraj
Recipe editor: Jennifer MacKenzie
Proofreader: Kelly Jones
Indexer: Gillian Watts
Photographer: Colin Ericson
Associate photographer: Matt Johannsson
Food stylist: Michael Elliott
Prop stylist: Charlene Ericson

Other photographs: Mosaic #1: Peanut Butter © istockphoto.com/BarnabyChambers; Patterned Bowls
© istockphoto.com/barol16; White Bowls © istockphoto.com/dkgilbey; Honey © istockphoto.com/
Materio; Mosaic #2: Spinach © istockphoto.com/Kativ; Oranges © istockphoto.com/Dimitris66; Dragon
Fruit © istockphoto.com/joakimbkk; Colorful Ceramic Bowls © istockphoto.com/jat306; Watermelon
© istockphoto.com/efired; Mixed Berries © istockphoto.com/TheRachelKay; Avocados © istockphoto.
com/FotografiaBasica; Mosaic #3: Tea Pot with Cups © istockphoto.com/DejanKolar; Coffee Beans
© istockphoto.com/BrianAJackson; Tea Leaves © istockphoto.com/Olha_Afanasieva; Kitchen Bowls
© istockphoto.com/Albuquerque.

Cover images (*clockwise from top*): Peach Paradise (page 114), Berry Banana Bowl (page 144), Pomegranate
Berry Bowl (page 163) and Green Coconut Bowl (page 83).

The publisher gratefully acknowledges the financial support of our publishing program by the
Government of Canada through the Canada Book Fund.

Published by Robert Rose Inc.
120 Eglinton Avenue East, Suite 800, Toronto, Ontario, Canada M4P 1E2
Tel: (416) 322-6552 Fax: (416) 322-6936
www.robertrose.ca

Printed and bound in Canada

1 2 3 4 5 6 7 8 9 MI 24 23 22 21 20 19 18 17 16

Contents

*To my husband, Doug Buettner, and
three kids, Alec, Leigh and Zachary.
You all are my life and love, and
I am so grateful for each of you!*

Acknowledgments

This book would not have been possible without many people. First, to Bob Dees, president of Robert Rose Inc., I am so grateful to you for believing in me and taking a chance on me again (the third time's the charm). I cannot thank you enough for being as excited about this project as I am.

Thanks to my editors, Sue Sumeraj and Jennifer MacKenzie, for their diligent and endless hours of work and helpful suggestions. To Martine Quibell, thanks for always being so helpful, supportive and lovely to work with. Thanks to everyone at PageWave Graphics, especially designer Kevin Cockburn, for making such a beautiful book and to Colin Erricson's photography team for the fabulous photographs.

Special thanks to Nancy Bynon for all of her help with recipe testing. She has been an amazing help for many years, continually offering wonderful ideas, suggestions and assistance.

A huge thanks goes out to all the people who tested recipes for me out of the goodness of their hearts and supported me, including Stephanie Lepore, Caroline Yeilding, Jamie Asman, Natalie and Eric Asman, Charles and Julie Stein, Peyton Hare, Heather Benamy, Emily Clark, Ana Sayers, Shirley Prince and especially my mother-in-law, Rosemary Buettner.

Most of all I have to thank my amazing husband, Doug Buettner, for his endless help with this book. His encouragement and help get me through every day. He is a gem, and I thank my lucky blessings every day to have him in my life. My three children, Alec, Leigh and Zachary, also helped me from start to finish on this project, grocery shopping, preparing recipes, offering ideas and tasting almost every recipe in this book. You are three incredibly fabulous children who make me smile and feel very proud every single day. You all are what life is all about, and I love you more than anything.

Introduction

When I told people in Alabama that I was working on a smoothie bowl cookbook, most of them asked, "What is a smoothie bowl?" If you are active on social media, especially Pinterest or Instagram, you won't need to ask that question. Smoothie bowls — thick smoothies that you eat with a spoon — are the latest breakfast trend. With smoothie bowls, you get the convenience, flavor and texture of a smoothie, but even more nutrition than liquid smoothies thanks to the addition of toppings such as fresh and dried fruits, seeds and nuts. Smoothie bowls are not just healthier but also more filling, as they give you something to chew (not just sip). They are often called "cereal 2.0," and they are the health world's new breakfast of choice — an easy way to get a good portion of your "five a day."

There are so many reasons to make smoothie bowls: they are tasty and pretty, kids love them, and they offer meal flexibility as you can eat one for breakfast or lunch, as a snack or even for dessert. They're an easy, time-friendly solution for those who feel they don't have time to eat many fruits and vegetables. But what I love most about them is that you get to be creative while preparing a meal or snack that is full of health benefits.

Health Benefits of Smoothie Bowls

The smoothie bowls in this book offer so many health benefits, but here are some of my favorites:

1. The recipes contain all-natural ingredients, most of which are raw, so they are packed with vitamins, minerals, phytonutrients and antioxidants.
2. They are made with natural superfoods, such as fruits, vegetables, nuts and seeds, that are high in dietary fiber, which aids digestion and keeps you feeling full for longer.
3. Many smoothie bowls contain anti-inflammatory foods such as blueberries, leafy greens, avocado, chia seeds, hemp seeds and walnuts.
4. Most of the recipes are loaded with vitamin C, which may help boost the immune system.
5. Many smoothie bowls include dairy products and other ingredients that are rich in calcium, which helps improve bone density and prevent osteoporosis. (If you use nondairy milk, make sure to purchase one that is fortified with calcium.)

Health Note

Most of the smoothie bowl recipes in this book are gluten-free and vegetarian, and many are appropriate for vegans.

Health Note

Fruits and vegetables provide a ton of energy, thanks to enzymes that allow for efficient digestion and absorption of food.

Choosing a Blender

Like smoothies, smoothie bowls are made using a blender. Choose one with a sturdy base and a tight-fitting lid. Make sure that it can chop firm fruits and vegetables, and that it is easy to clean. Any blender will work for recipes made with fresh fruit, but for frozen fruit, you're better off with a high-powered blender, such as a Vitamix or Nutribullet. Leafy greens are also more difficult to blend well in a regular blender.

Here are some other considerations when buying a blender:

- **Capacity:** Most new blenders hold between 2 and 8 cups (500 mL and 2 L). The recipes in this book make 1 to 2 servings (usually around 1 to 3 cups/250 to 750 mL), but they can be doubled. If you plan to make larger batches most of the time, consider a blender with a capacity on the larger side.
- **Materials:** Blenders may be made of plastic, glass or stainless steel. Plastic is less expensive but may wear out more quickly. Glass is easy to clean and dishwasher-safe, and will not wear out over time. Stainless steel is easy to clean and keeps mixtures cold but is the most expensive.
- **Settings:** Ice crushing and pulse settings are nice features, but are not necessary for the recipes in this book.

How to Build a Smoothie Bowl

There is a science to building a smoothie bowl. To ensure the best results, add the ingredients to the blender in the following order:

1. **Liquids:** First, add your liquid ingredients, such as yogurt, milk, juice, coffee or tea.
2. **Powders:** Next, add any powders, such as protein powder or cocoa powder, so they don't get trapped at the bottom or top. Ground flax seeds (flaxseed meal) and ground spices also fall into this category. Rolled oats, while not a powder, also work best added here.
3. **Hard ingredients:** After the powders, add hard ingredients, such as frozen fruit, nuts and seeds.
4. **Softer ingredients:** Next, add softer ingredients, such as greens, fresh fruits and vegetables, nut butters and fresh herbs.
5. **Ice:** Add ice last, and only when you're sure you're going to need it to make your smoothie bowl nice and thick. If the recipe includes a number of hard ingredients, blend without ice first, to make sure they are well blended and incorporated, then blend in the ice.

The Smoothie Bowl Pantry

The key to success when creating a delicious, nutritious smoothie bowl is to use the freshest, most natural ingredients possible. Fresh fruits and vegetables — or fruits and vegetables frozen at their peak of freshness — are, of course, the stars of the show. But look for the highest-quality, least-processed versions of all other ingredients as well: your payoff will be good taste and good health.

Yogurt and Kefir

Both regular and Greek yogurt are used in the recipes in this book, in both plain and flavored versions. Regular and Greek yogurt are both healthy choices, filled with protein and probiotics, but Greek yogurt is strained to remove the whey, creating a creamier, thicker texture that is wonderful in smoothie bowls. Greek yogurt also typically has more protein than regular yogurt.

Kefir is similar to liquid yogurt and is thicker than milk. It is high in protein, calcium, vitamin D and probiotics, and adds a tangy flavor to smoothie bowls.

Ice Cream and Frozen Yogurt

Many of the recipes in the Dessert Bowls chapter and some in the Coffee and Tea Smoothie Bowls chapter use ice cream or frozen yogurt (either regular or Greek). For easier blending, add ice cream and frozen yogurt after more liquid ingredients.

Milk and Nondairy Milk

Many smoothie bowl recipes include milk, whether dairy or nondairy. In most cases, you can use any milk you prefer, substituting one for another as you please. Keep in mind, though, that the recipes have been balanced for sweetness based on the milk specified; if you substitute a different type of milk, you may have sweeter or less sweet results.

I most often use cow's milk, almond milk, soy milk or coconut milk beverage in my recipes. You can choose from among these or use another milk you prefer, such as hemp milk or rice milk.

Cow's Milk

You can use dairy milk with any fat level in smoothie bowls. I personally prefer to use nonfat (skim) milk, but regular or low-fat milk will work equally well. If you cannot digest

Health Note

Probiotics are "good" bacteria that support the immune system, aid in digestive issues and have a positive effect on the brain and mental health. They are plentiful in both yogurt and kefir, and are listed in the ingredients as "live active cultures."

lactose, lactose-reduced milk can be substituted successfully. If you choose to use an organic milk, make sure it's fortified with calcium and vitamin D.

Almond Milk

Almond milk gives smoothies a nutty taste and creamy texture. It comes sweetened or unsweetened, and in plain and flavored versions. I most often use unsweetened almond milk, either plain or vanilla-flavored, but occasionally call for sweetened almond milk. If you substitute sweetened milk for unsweetened, or vice versa, be aware that the sweetness balance of the recipe will change.

Soy Milk

Soy milk is a bit higher in healthy unsaturated fats than other nondairy milks, and it adds a rich flavor to smoothie bowls. It is lactose-free and a good source of protein and calcium. Like almond milk, soy milk comes sweetened or unsweetened, and in plain and flavored versions. If you substitute sweetened milk for unsweetened, or vice versa, be aware that the sweetness balance of the recipe will change.

Coconut Milk Beverage

Coconut milk beverage comes in a carton and can be found in the dairy section of the grocery store. It has a fresh coconut flavor that perks up smoothie bowls. It is lactose-free and is a good source of vitamins D and B_{12}, but is low in protein.

Make sure to use coconut milk beverage in these recipes; canned coconut milk is much thicker and will create dramatically different results.

Coconut Water

When purchasing coconut water, be sure to read labels. Avoid coconut water from concentrate and any that has additives, sweeteners or unusual ingredients.

Other Liquids

Just about any liquid can be used to thin and flavor smoothie bowls, from water to juice to coffee or tea (see the dedicated chapter on coffee and tea smoothie bowls, pages 169–188).

In addition, you may also want to use smaller amounts of liquid flavorings, such as sweeteners, vanilla extract or freshly squeezed lemon or lime juice. When it comes to sweeteners, my personal preference is honey, but agave syrup and pure maple syrup are also good options. You can use an equal amount of maple syrup or agave syrup in any recipe that calls for honey.

If a recipe calls for both grated citrus zest and citrus juice, don't forget to zest the citrus fruit before juicing it. You can add the zest and the juice together, with the other liquids.

Protein Powder

Many of these recipes include protein powder to help make them more nutritionally complete, perfect when you need a quick healthy breakfast or to help your body recover and rebuild after a workout. There are many protein powders out there, from whey to casein to soy, and you should simply choose the one that is best suited to your dietary needs and specific goals. Most of the smoothie bowls use unflavored protein powder, but a handful call for vanilla- or chocolate-flavored protein powder.

You can add protein powder to any smoothie bowl recipe. Just keep in mind that it should always be blended with the liquid ingredients before any of the remaining ingredients are added.

Ground Flax Seeds

Because the recipes in this book use ground flax seeds (flaxseed meal) rather than whole seeds, they are treated like a powder and added after the liquids. If you are using a high-powered blender, you can substitute whole flax seeds, but blend them with the liquids first, before adding the remaining ingredients.

Ground or whole flax seeds also make a terrific topping for smoothie bowls.

Store ground flax seeds in an airtight container in the refrigerator. Whole flax seeds can be stored in an airtight container in a cool, dark, dry spot.

Cocoa Powder

Just a small amount of unsweetened cocoa powder adds incredible chocolate flavor to smoothie bowls. Although any unsweetened cocoa powder will work, I prefer to use raw cacao powder for the best flavor and least processing.

Health Note

Flax seeds are a rich source of dietary fiber, manganese, vitamin B_1 and omega-3 fatty acids. Just 2 tbsp (30 mL) of ground flax seeds contains more than 140% of the daily value of omega-3s and more lignans than any other plant food. One tablespoon (15 mL) contains 55 calories, 3 grams of carbohydrate, 2.8 grams of fiber, 1.9 grams of protein and 4.3 grams of fat.

Ground Spices

Small amounts of ground spices can add a huge amount of flavor to your smoothie bowls. My favorites include cinnamon, cardamom and nutmeg.

Oats

Oats in a smoothie bowl? They are actually a great addition, adding flavor, bulk and nutrition. The best oats to use in smoothie bowl recipes are large-flake (old-fashioned) rolled oats. Add them after the liquids and before the hard ingredients.

Creamier Smoothie Bowls

To make smoothies creamier, try adding one or more of these ingredients:

- Avocado
- Banana
- Cooked grains, such as quinoa or oatmeal
- Frozen fruit
- Nut butter
- Nut, rice or soy milk
- Rolled grains, such as oats or quinoa flakes
- Shredded coconut
- Soft tofu
- Virgin coconut oil
- Yogurt (regular or Greek)

Frozen Fruits

Once the liquids and powders are in the blender, the next thing to add is your frozen fruit. Any frozen fruit makes a great addition to a smoothie bowl. The more frozen fruit you use, the thicker your smoothie will be and the less likely you will need to add any ice.

Although frozen fruits and fresh fruits are essentially interchangeable in smoothie bowl recipes, keep in mind that the consistency of the smoothie will change with the substitution, and you will need to adjust the amount of ice to compensate.

Check your grocery store to see what types of frozen fruits they stock. There's an astonishing variety out there and, conveniently, they're already chopped or sliced — less work for you! In addition to packages of individual fruits, keep your eye out for ready-made fruit and fruit-and-vegetable mixes; they're a great way to add a variety of flavors to a recipe with a minimum of effort.

You can, of course, also freeze your own fresh fruit at home, and in the case of bananas, you will want to do this on a regular basis, so you always have frozen bananas on hand for smoothie bowl recipes.

I've highlighted a couple of the more unusual frozen fruits below, as well as some good options for home freezing.

Açaí

Açaí has a beautiful purple-eggplant color and tastes like a combination of blueberries and chocolate. Purchase frozen açaí purée in packages at gourmet grocery stores, online or at health food stores. Be sure to buy pure, unsweetened purée.

Bananas

The vast majority of the recipes in this book use a frozen banana to create a rich, frosty smoothie. You can freeze either ripe or overripe bananas — it's a great way to salvage those overripe ones!

- **If you have a high-powered blender:** Peel the bananas, leaving some whole and cutting some in half (for recipes that call for $\frac{1}{2}$ banana). Seal up to 6 bananas in a large freezer bag.
- **If you do not have a high-powered blender:** Peel the bananas and cut each one into small pieces. Seal the pieces in individual freezer bags in portioned amounts (one banana's worth of pieces; one-half banana's worth of pieces).
- You can store bananas in the freezer for up to 3 months. Remove them from the freezer immediately before adding them to the blender, so they don't have time to thaw.

Berries

Freezing your own berries is easy and economical when fresh berries are in season. To freeze berries, remove the stems (if applicable) and spread the berries out on a baking sheet. Freeze for 2 hours or until completely frozen. Transfer to an airtight container and freeze for up to 6 months. This method will prevent the frozen berries from clumping together.

Dragon Fruit

Look for frozen dragon fruit at specialty grocery stores, Asian markets or online. Before using it, remove it from the freezer and let it stand for a few minutes, then cut the package open and squeeze out the fruit.

Health Note

Açaí is high in antioxidants and is a good source of fiber.

Caution

If you do not have a high-powered blender, be sure to use cut-up pieces of frozen banana rather than adding a whole or halved frozen banana to the blender.

Health Note

Dragon fruit is a good source of vitamin C, fiber and iron. It also provides 2 grams of protein per 200 grams, which is a lot for a fruit!

Berry Healthy

Whether fresh or frozen, berries are one of the easiest, tastiest and most colorful additions to a smoothie bowl — and they make great toppings, too. So how perfect is it that they're also true superfoods, simply packed with good nutrition.

- **Blackberries:** With one of the highest antioxidant contents per serving of any food, blackberries have a positive impact on athletic activity. They also contain anthocyanin, which protects the brain from stress and reduces the effects of Alzheimer's disease. Blackberries provide 7 grams of fiber per cup (250 mL) — the most fiber of all the berries.
- **Blueberries:** Blueberries contain antioxidants that can improve vision, improve memory and reduce the risk of infections. They are a good source of fiber and vitamin C.
- **Cranberries:** These Thanksgiving staples are loaded with antioxidants and vitamin C, and they contain antibacterial compounds that are believed to help prevent urinary tract infections.
- **Raspberries:** Raspberries provide phytonutrients that can increase the metabolism in fat cells, decreasing the risk of obesity and improving heart health. They are also high in anti-inflammatory antioxidants.
- **Strawberries:** Rich in vitamin C, fiber and potassium, strawberries are also an excellent source of folate, which is essential for a healthy immune system. Like raspberries, strawberries have a high phytonutrient content that contributes to heart health.

Nuts and Seeds

A wide variety of nuts and seeds is used in the recipes in this book, either in the smoothie bowls themselves or as a topping. Choose unsalted nuts and seeds for smoothie bowls. Some good options to keep on hand include almonds, walnuts, pecans, cashews, chia seeds, hemp seeds, sunflower seeds and green pumpkin seeds (pepitas).

Soaking Nuts and Seeds

If you don't have a high-powered blender — or if you simply prefer your smoothies to have a less crunchy texture — you will want to soak nuts and certain seeds before adding them to the blender (or before toasting them).

- **For nuts:** Place the nuts in a bowl, cover with warm water and let soak for 20 to 30 minutes. Drain well before adding to the blender.
- **For sunflower and pumpkin seeds:** Place the seeds in a bowl with twice as much warm water by volume and let soak for at least 1 hour. Drain well before adding to the blender.

Toasting Nuts and Seeds

Toasting nuts and seeds brings out great flavor and adds crunch. Toast them in a dry skillet over medium heat, stirring frequently, until golden brown. Alternatively, toast them in a preheated 350°F (180°C) oven, stirring occasionally, for 5 to 15 minutes (depending on size) or until golden brown. Let cool completely before adding them to the blender.

Greens

Greens work best in smoothie bowl recipes in combination with other vegetables, fruits and/or herbs. Some of my favorite greens to use are kale, spinach and arugula. Greens are so nutritious, and so fabulous in smoothie bowls, I've devoted a whole chapter to Green Creations (pages 57–96)!

Fresh Fruits and Vegetables

Fresh fruits are a great option for smoothie bowls when they are in season and at their peak of freshness. Keep in mind that your smoothie will be less thick when you use fresh fruit, and you will need more ice than you would with frozen fruit.

While I can't think of a single fresh fruit that wouldn't be fantastic in a smoothie bowl, there are a smaller number of vegetables that work well. In addition to greens, the recipes in this book use celery, seedless cucumber, cooked beets, carrots and pumpkin purée.

Simple Smoothie Substitutions

You're getting ready to whip up a smoothie bowl when you realize you're missing a key ingredient. What to do? Well, in many cases, you can simply substitute something else. Here are some quick fixes that will work well.

- Any type of milk — dairy or nondairy — may be substituted for the milk specified in the recipe. Keep in mind, though, that the recipes have been balanced for sweetness based on the milk specified; if you substitute a different type of milk, you may have sweeter or less sweet results.
- If you don't have coconut water, replace it with water. (Or replace water with coconut water to add more flavor to a recipe.)

- Replace any frozen fruit with fresh fruit, but use more ice.
- Replace any fresh fruit with frozen fruit, but use less ice.
- Substitute plain yogurt for vanilla-flavored yogurt, and vice versa. But keep in mind that flavored yogurts contain more sugar, which will affect the sweetness balance in the recipe.
- Use an equal amount of agave syrup or pure maple syrup in place of honey.

Dried Fruits

Dried fruits deliver a concentrated hit of flavor and nutrients, whether added to the smoothie itself or sprinkled on as a topping. If you don't have a high-powered blender, be sure to soak dried fruits before adding them to the blender. First, finely chop any large dried fruits, such as apricots. Add the dried fruits to the measured liquid called for in the recipe and soak for 15 to 20 minutes or until the fruit begins to plump. Add the fruit and liquid to the blender.

Nut and Peanut Butters

Nut and peanut butters add flavor, protein and creaminess to smoothie bowls. Although nuts are added to the blender with the frozen fruits, nut butters are added later, with the softer ingredients.

Making homemade nut butters is easy and can be less expensive. I have included five nut butter recipes in the Toppings chapter (pages 207–231). If you opt for store-bought instead, choose unsalted nut butters.

For peanut butter, I personally prefer to use a natural peanut butter with no added sugar or oil, but any peanut butter will work fine in smoothie bowl recipes.

Herbs

Fresh herbs add a fresh flavor, antioxidants and vitamins to smoothie bowls. Basil, mint, parsley and cilantro are some of my favorite additions. Add them last, just before the ice, and/ or sprinkle them on top of your smoothie bowl.

Ice

The recipes in this book call for ice cubes, but feel free to use crushed ice instead. To replace 4 ice cubes, you'll need about ½ to ⅓ cup (125 to 175 mL) crushed ice. Add it a little bit at a time, blending until your desired consistency is achieved.

If a recipe calls for a set amount of ice (typically 4 cubes), that is the amount I found worked best in combination with the other ingredients. But the consistency of the smoothie bowl is always up to you, and you can use more or less ice to get the texture you're looking for.

If the recipe does not specify an amount of ice, it's because there are variables in the recipe that make the resulting consistency uncertain (whether you choose fresh or frozen fruit, for example); in those cases, you will want to check the consistency after blending all of the other ingredients to determine whether you need ice at all. If you do, add it one cube at a time, blending each cube until smooth and checking the consistency again before adding the next one.

Flavored Ice Cubes

You can freeze any liquid into ice cubes, and using flavored ice will take your smoothie bowls to the next level. Keep in mind that the higher the sugar content, the softer the ice will be. And note that all flavored ice melts more quickly than ice cubes made with water.

Try making ice cubes from chocolate milk, almond milk, coconut milk beverage, coconut water, tea or coffee — or any other liquid you're using in a recipe. Freeze the liquid in an ice cube tray until solid, then transfer the cubes to an airtight container. The cubes will keep for several months.

Detox Ice Cubes

Perfect for summer hydration, detox ice cubes are a simple way to infuse water-based ice cubes with flavor. Cut fruit (raspberries, strawberries, blueberries, lemons, limes, grapefruit, oranges) and/or herbs (fresh basil or mint) into pieces small enough to fit in an ice cube tray. Distribute the fruit and/or herbs in the tray, add water and freeze. Use in smoothie bowls for an added hit of flavor.

Watermelon Cubes

Watermelon cubes are another great alternative to ice cubes, or can be used to replace fresh or frozen chopped watermelon in smoothie bowl recipes. Slice a seedless watermelon into cubes. Spread the cubes in an even layer on a baking sheet, cover with plastic wrap and freeze for 3 hours or until completely frozen. Transfer the cubes to an airtight container and store in the freezer for up to 2 weeks. They're not just great for smoothies — enjoy them as a healthy snack or add them to water or your favorite summer beverage.

Creative Variation

When making detox ice cubes to use for chilling beverages, create a beautiful striped look by alternate freezing layers of water with layers of fruit and herbs.

Smoothie Bowl Toppings

Where the science of blending ingredients ends, the art of topping your smoothie bowl begins! Toppings are what take these recipes from smoothie to smoothie bowl. They add color, flavor, texture and nutrition, and they allow each diner to customize their own bowl, creating their own edible work of art.

The topping possibilities are endless, and you can be as creative as you like in mixing and matching your flavors and textures. Here are some of my favorites:

- Ground spices
- Unsweetened cocoa powder
- Chopped or sliced fresh fruit
- Dried fruit
- Shredded or flaked coconut

- Granola
- Chocolate chips
- Nuts
- Seeds
- Chopped fresh herbs

Top 10 Tips for Success

1. To make a thicker smoothie, use as much frozen fruit as possible. To make a thinner smoothie, add more liquid.

2. Purchase fresh fruits and vegetables that are in season and at their peak of freshness, and use them as soon as possible. For fruits that are out of season locally, use frozen.

3. When using fruits with a high water content, such as watermelon or oranges, don't use as much liquid.

4. Juice your own fruits and vegetables and use the juice in your smoothie.

5. Instead of a sweetener such as honey, use dates to sweeten your smoothie. Soak them in the liquid you plan to use in your recipe for 15 to 20 minutes before blending.

6. Always taste your smoothie before pouring it into a bowl; you might want to make small flavor or texture additions.

7. If your smoothie is too sweet, add more ice, water or greens. Conversely, if you're using bitter greens, balance them with sweet fruits.

8. Pour your smoothie into thick-rimmed cereal or soup bowls. A thinner bowl will hasten the melting time.

9. Always have your toppings prepared ahead of time so you can add them to your smoothie bowl before it starts to melt.

10. Serve smoothie bowls immediately or freeze them for a few minutes.

Smoothie Troubleshooting

Issue: My smoothie is too thin.

Solution: Add a thickening ingredient, such as protein powder, avocado, frozen fruit or ice. The next time you make the smoothie, try reducing the amount of liquid.

Issue: My smoothie is too thick.

Solution: Add more liquid, stir it in with a spoon and blend again. Keep adding liquid until you achieve the desired consistency.

Issue: My smoothie mixture is not blending well.

Solution: If frozen or hard fruits and vegetables get stuck, remove them and add liquid, then return them gradually to the blender, blending after each addition. For future smoothies, make sure to blend the liquids and hard ingredients first, before adding any remaining ingredients. Add more liquid if you are still having a difficult time getting the mixture to blend.

Filling your blender jar too high may also cause blending issues. If making a large batch, add ingredients gradually, blending each addition until smooth before adding more.

Issue: My smoothie is not sweet enough.

Solution: Add honey, agave syrup, pure maple syrup or soaked dates. Stir the sweetener into the smoothie, then blend again.

Issue: My smoothie has a bitter taste.

Solution: Add more liquid and/or more fruit.

Issue: My smoothie mixture is an unattractive color.

Solution: Hide it with an array of colorful smoothie toppings. And be assured that it will taste better than it looks!

Issue: The recipe only makes 2 servings and I want to make smoothies for 4 people.

Solution: You can easily double any recipe in this book. Just make sure to use a full-size blender with a large-enough capacity.

Breakfast Smoothie Bowls

Complete Breakfast Smoothie Bowl

This breakfast smoothie has it all: protein, carbohydrates, fiber, antioxidants, vitamins and minerals.

MAKES 2 SERVINGS

Tip

Shredded coconut is full of flavor and makes a healthy snack. Use it to decorate cakes and pies, or add it to granola or trail mix.

1½ cups	plain or vanilla-flavored Greek yogurt	375 mL
1 tsp	ground flax seeds (flaxseed meal)	5 mL
½	frozen banana, cut into pieces if necessary (see page 14)	½
½ cup	sliced peaches	125 mL
	Ice cubes	

SUGGESTED TOPPINGS

Blueberries

Raspberries

Golden raisins

Dried cranberries

Unsweetened shredded coconut

Chopped pecans

Ground flax seeds (flaxseed meal)

1. In blender, combine yogurt, flax seeds, banana and peaches. Secure lid and blend (from low to high if using a variable-speed blender) until smooth. Add ice, one cube at a time, blending until the desired consistency is achieved.

2. Pour into bowls and top with any of the suggested toppings, as desired.

Breakfast Harvest Bowl

This smoothie will fill you up, so you will be less hungry throughout the day. Add ½ tsp (2 mL) ground flax seeds (flaxseed meal) with the protein powder for more omega-3 fatty acids.

**MAKES
1 SERVING**

¼ cup	unsweetened apple juice	60 mL
1 tsp	liquid honey	5 mL
1 tsp	protein powder	5 mL
½ cup	frozen blackberries	125 mL
½	ripe banana	½
1 cup	chopped plums	250 mL
	Ice cubes	

SUGGESTED TOPPINGS

Sliced banana

Blackberries

Sliced plums

Easy Muesli (page 219)

1. In blender, combine apple juice, honey and protein powder. Secure lid and blend (from low to high if using a variable-speed blender) until smooth. Add blackberries, banana and plums; blend until smooth. Add ice, one cube at a time, blending until the desired consistency is achieved.

2. Pour into a bowl and top with any of the suggested toppings, as desired.

Variation

If plums are not in season, substitute 1 cup (250 mL) frozen sliced peaches and omit the ice.

Breakfast Starter

This recipe has a great supply of protein, so you'll feel energized throughout the day.

MAKES 1 SERVING

Tips

Any flavor of soy milk may be used.

Protein powder is a great way to add protein to your diet, especially in the morning. It is beneficial for those who do not consume an adequate amount of protein, such as vegetarians, and can help your body recharge and build muscle after a workout.

You can use store-bought granola or any of the granola recipes in this book (pages 210–218) to top your smoothie bowl.

1 cup	unsweetened soy milk	250 mL
1 tsp	liquid honey	5 mL
1 tbsp	protein powder	15 mL
1	frozen banana, cut into pieces if necessary (see page 14)	1
1 cup	strawberries	250 mL
	Ice cubes	

SUGGESTED TOPPINGS

Sliced banana

Sliced strawberries

Granola

Ground hemp seeds

Ground flax seeds (flaxseed meal)

Wheat germ

1. In blender, combine soy milk, honey and protein powder. Secure lid and blend (from low to high if using a variable-speed blender) until smooth. Add banana and strawberries; blend until smooth. Add ice, one cube at a time, blending until the desired consistency is achieved.

2. Pour into a bowl and top with any of the suggested toppings, as desired.

Breakfast to Go

Coconut water is helpful for rehydration. If you sweat a lot or take hot yoga classes, it's a great addition to your diet.

MAKES 1 SERVING

Tip

Keep bananas in the freezer so you always have them on hand to make nice thick smoothie bowls.

½ cup	plain Greek yogurt	125 mL
¼ cup	coconut water	60 mL
1 tsp	liquid honey	5 mL
¼ tsp	ground flax seeds (flaxseed meal)	1 mL
½	frozen banana, cut into pieces if necessary (see page 14)	½
¼ cup	frozen strawberries	60 mL
¼ cup	prunes	60 mL
	Ice cubes (optional)	

SUGGESTED TOPPINGS

Sliced strawberries
Sliced banana
Kitchen Sink Granola (page 218)
Ground flax seeds (flaxseed meal)

1. In blender, combine yogurt, coconut water, honey, flax seeds, banana, strawberries and prunes. Secure lid and blend (from low to high if using a variable-speed blender) until smooth. If a thicker consistency is desired, add ice, one cube at a time, and blend until smooth.

2. Pour into a bowl and top with any of the suggested toppings, as desired.

Variation

Substitute ¼ cup (60 mL) dried figs or apricots for the prunes.

Bowl of Health

Cardamom, one of the main ingredients in chai tea, is a great addition to this morning smoothie bowl.

**MAKES 1 TO
2 SERVINGS**

Tips

This recipe is also great with 1 tbsp (15 mL) peanut butter or Homemade Almond Butter (page 226). Add it after the banana.

Purchase sunflower seeds already shelled and without salt.

½ cup	coconut water	125 mL
1 tsp	ground flax seeds (flaxseed meal)	5 mL
1 tsp	ground cinnamon	5 mL
1 tsp	ground cardamom	5 mL
1	frozen banana, cut into pieces if necessary (see page 14)	1
¼ cup	sunflower seeds	60 mL
4	ice cubes	4

SUGGESTED TOPPINGS

Ground cinnamon

Sliced banana

Unsweetened shredded coconut

Coconut Granola (page 216)

Chopped nuts

Sunflower seeds

1. In blender, combine coconut water, flax seeds, cinnamon, cardamom, banana, sunflower seeds and ice. Secure lid and blend (from low to high if using a variable-speed blender) until smooth.

2. Pour into a bowl or bowls and top with any of the suggested toppings, as desired.

Peanut Butter Oat Bowl

This recipe is fast and simple to prepare on busy mornings. It will fill you up, so it's ideal for days when you know you won't be eating lunch until late in the day.

**MAKES
1 SERVING**

Tip

If you don't have a frozen banana, use a ripe banana and more ice.

¾ cup	unsweetened almond milk	175 mL
2 tbsp	large-flake (old-fashioned) rolled oats	30 mL
½ tsp	ground cinnamon	2 mL
1	frozen banana, cut into pieces if necessary (see page 14)	1
1 tbsp	peanut butter	15 mL
4	ice cubes	4

SUGGESTED TOPPINGS

Ground cinnamon

Sliced banana

Rolled oats

Peanut Butter Granola (page 212)

1. In blender, combine almond milk, oats, cinnamon, banana, peanut butter and ice. Secure lid and blend (from low to high if using a variable-speed blender) until smooth.

2. Pour into a bowl and top with any of the suggested toppings, as desired.

Variation

Substitute Cinnamon Cashew Nut Butter (page 228) for the peanut butter.

Peanut Butter Quinoa Bowl

Quinoa, peanut butter, banana and honey create a delicious and nutritious breakfast.

**MAKES
1 SERVING**

Tips

Purchase pre-rinsed quinoa to ease preparation and avoid a bitter flavor. If you're not sure whether it's pre-rinsed, rinse it under cool running water in a sieve before cooking.

You can use store-bought granola or any of the granola recipes in this book (pages 210–218) to top your smoothie bowl.

⅓ cup	unsweetened almond milk	75 mL
2 tsp	liquid honey	10 mL
1	frozen banana, cut into pieces if necessary (see page 14)	1
½ cup	cooled cooked quinoa	125 mL
¼ cup	peanut butter	60 mL
4	ice cubes	4

SUGGESTED TOPPINGS

Sliced banana

Cooked quinoa or toasted raw quinoa

Granola

Peanuts

Hemp seeds

1. In blender, combine almond milk, honey, banana, quinoa, peanut butter and ice. Secure lid and blend (from low to high if using a variable-speed blender) until smooth.

2. Pour into a bowl and top with any of the suggested toppings, as desired.

Variations

Substitute Homemade Almond Butter (page 226) for the peanut butter.

If you don't have cooked quinoa on hand, prepare ¼ cup (60 mL) uncooked large-flake (old-fashioned) rolled oats according to package directions and use in place of the quinoa.

PB&J Bowl

A twist on a peanut butter and jelly sandwich, this recipe is one of my son's favorites.

Tip

Wash strawberries well in cold water and pat dry. To freeze them, remove the stems and spread them out on a baking sheet. Freeze for 2 hours or until completely frozen. Transfer to an airtight container and freeze for up to 6 months. This method will prevent the frozen berries from clumping together.

¼ cup	milk	60 mL
1 tbsp	protein powder	15 mL
½ cup	frozen strawberries	125 mL
2 tbsp	peanut butter	30 mL
1 tbsp	strawberry jelly	15 mL
	Ice cubes (optional)	

SUGGESTED TOPPINGS

Strawberries

Sliced banana

Peanut Butter Granola (page 212)

1. In blender, combine milk and protein powder. Secure lid and blend (from low to high if using a variable-speed blender) until smooth. Add strawberries, peanut butter and jelly; blend until smooth. If a thicker consistency is desired, add ice, one cube at a time, and blend until smooth.

2. Pour into a bowl and top with any of the suggested toppings, as desired.

Variation

Almond Butter and Jelly Bowl: Substitute Homemade Almond Butter (page 226) for the peanut butter.

Frosty French Toast

Everyone's favorite classic French toast breakfast is now healthier in this smoothie bowl.

Tip

Add frozen banana to your blender in pieces to make blending easier and faster.

½ cup	unsweetened vanilla-flavored soy milk	125 mL
1 tbsp	pure maple syrup	15 mL
1 tsp	vanilla extract	5 mL
2 tsp	ground flax seeds (flaxseed meal)	10 mL
1 tsp	ground cinnamon	5 mL
½ tsp	ground nutmeg	2 mL
1	frozen banana, cut into pieces if necessary (see page 14)	1
4	ice cubes	4

SUGGESTED TOPPINGS

Ground cinnamon or nutmeg
Sliced banana
Spiced Pecans (page 221)
Ground flax seeds (flaxseed meal)

1. In blender, combine soy milk, maple syrup, vanilla, flax seeds, cinnamon, nutmeg, banana and ice. Secure lid and blend (from low to high if using a variable-speed blender) until smooth.

2. Pour into a bowl and top with any of the suggested toppings, as desired.

Variation

Substitute any type of milk for the soy milk, and replace the maple syrup with liquid honey.

Cinnamon Roll Smoothie Bowl

Cinnamon is the star of this creation, a light twist on the baked version.

MAKES 1 SERVING			

½ cup	vanilla-flavored Greek yogurt	125 mL
1 tsp	liquid honey	5 mL
2 tsp	protein powder	10 mL
1 tsp	ground cinnamon	5 mL
¼ tsp	ground flax seeds (flaxseed meal)	1 mL
1	frozen banana, cut into pieces if necessary (see page 14)	1
4	ice cubes	4

SUGGESTED TOPPINGS

Ground cinnamon

Maple Cinnamon Granola (page 211)

Pecan halves or chopped pecans

Ground flax seeds (flaxseed meal)

1. In blender, combine yogurt, honey and protein powder. Secure lid and blend (from low to high if using a variable-speed blender) until smooth. Add cinnamon, flax seeds, banana and ice; blend until smooth.

2. Pour into a bowl and top with any of the suggested toppings, as desired.

Variation

Add a ¼-inch (0.5 cm) piece of fresh vanilla bean or 1 tsp (5 mL) vanilla extract.

Mixed Fruit and Greek Yogurt Bowl

Greek yogurt flavored with honey is a tasty liquid starter, and adds a protein boost to start off your day on the right foot.

MAKES 1 TO 2 SERVINGS

Tips

Use a frozen fruit mix with chopped peaches, strawberries and bananas, such as Dole ready-cut frozen fruit, or simply use ½ cup (125 mL) of each fruit.

If you like your smoothie bowl extra sweet, add 1 tsp (5 mL) liquid honey.

½ cup	honey-sweetened Greek yogurt	125 mL
¼ cup	milk	60 mL
½	frozen banana, cut into pieces if necessary (see page 14)	½
1½ cups	frozen mixed chopped peaches, strawberries and bananas	375 mL
1 cup	frozen chopped pineapple	250 mL
	Ice cubes (optional)	

SUGGESTED TOPPINGS

Sliced banana

Sliced peaches

Sliced strawberries

Dried pineapple pieces

Kitchen Sink Granola (page 218)

1. In blender, combine yogurt, milk, banana, mixed fruit and pineapple. Secure lid and blend (from low to high if using a variable-speed blender) until smooth. If a thicker consistency is desired, add ice, one cube at a time, and blend until smooth.

2. Pour into a bowl or bowls and top with any of the suggested toppings, as desired.

Blueberry Detox

Fresh orange zest and ginger balance nicely with peaches and blueberries to create wellness in a bowl.

○○○

**MAKES
2 SERVINGS**

Tips

To store gingerroot, leave it unpeeled and store in a plastic storage bag in the refrigerator.

If you use frozen blueberries, you will not need to add any ice.

You can use store-bought granola or any of the granola recipes in this book (pages 210–218) to top your smoothie bowl.

2 tbsp	freshly squeezed orange juice	30 mL
1 tbsp	freshly squeezed lemon juice	15 mL
1 tbsp	water	15 mL
2 tsp	liquid honey	10 mL
1	frozen banana, cut into pieces if necessary (see page 14)	1
½ cup	frozen sliced peaches	125 mL
1 cup	blueberries	250 mL
1 tsp	grated orange zest	5 mL
1 tsp	grated gingerroot	5 mL
	Ice cubes (optional)	

SUGGESTED TOPPINGS

Blueberries

Sliced banana

Grated orange zest

Granola

Ground flax seeds (flaxseed meal)

1. In blender, combine orange juice, lemon juice, water, honey, banana, peaches, blueberries, orange zest and ginger. Secure lid and blend (from low to high if using a variable-speed blender) until smooth. If a thicker consistency is desired, add ice, one cube at a time, and blend until smooth.

2. Pour into bowls and top with any of the suggested toppings, as desired.

· ·

Variation

Add 1 scoop of protein powder for added thickness and protein. Blend it with the liquids before adding the remaining ingredients.

Blueberry Banana Bowl

Kick your day off with this recipe — it's packed with protein and two of my favorite healthy seeds.

○○

**MAKES
2 SERVINGS**

Tip

To freeze blueberries, spread them out in a single layer on a baking sheet. Freeze for 2 hours or until completely frozen. Transfer to an airtight container and freeze for up to 6 months. This method will prevent the frozen berries from clumping together.

½ cup	unsweetened almond milk	125 mL
½	scoop vanilla-flavored protein powder	½
½ tsp	chia seeds	2 mL
½ tsp	ground flax seeds (flaxseed meal)	2 mL
1	frozen banana, cut into pieces if necessary (see page 14)	1
1 cup	blueberries (fresh or frozen)	250 mL
	Ice cubes (optional)	

SUGGESTED TOPPINGS

Blueberries

Banana Chips (page 208)

Healthy Trail Mix (page 220)

1. In blender, combine almond milk and protein powder. Secure lid and blend (from low to high if using a variable-speed blender) until smooth. Add chia seeds, flax seeds, banana and blueberries; blend until smooth. If a thicker consistency is desired, add ice, one cube at a time, and blend until smooth.

2. Pour into bowls and top with any of the suggested toppings, as desired.

Variation

Substitute your favorite milk for the almond milk in this recipe.

A.M. Goji Berry Bowl

When purchasing dried goji berries, look for those with a strong red color. Their cranberry-like flavor pairs well with the frozen berries in this recipe.

Tip

Look for goji berries at specialty food stores, well-stocked grocery stores and health food stores. They sometimes come in a resealable package. If not, store them in an airtight container. They do not need to be stored in the refrigerator, but they will last longer if they are refrigerated.

½ cup	plain Greek yogurt	125 mL
¼ cup	freshly squeezed orange juice	60 mL
2 tsp	liquid honey	10 mL
2 cups	frozen mixed berries	500 mL
½ cup	goji berries	125 mL

SUGGESTED TOPPINGS

Blueberries
Sliced strawberries
Classic Granola (page 210)
Ground flax seeds (flaxseed meal)

1. In blender, combine yogurt, orange juice, honey, mixed berries and goji berries. Secure lid and blend (from low to high if using a variable-speed blender) until smooth.

2. Pour into a bowl and top with any of the suggested toppings, as desired.

Variations

Add 1 tbsp (15 mL) protein powder after the honey for additional protein and thickness. Blend it with the liquids before adding the remaining ingredients.

Use ½ cup (125 mL) flavored Greek yogurt instead of the plain yogurt, and reduce the honey to 1 tsp (5 mL).

Use fresh berries instead of frozen and add 4 ice cubes.

Substitute unsweetened apple juice for the orange juice.

Raspberry Peach Bowl

Raspberries have just 65 calories per cup (250 mL), so pile them on top of this smoothie bowl.

Tip

If you have leftover ripe peaches and want to freeze them, first blanch and peel them. To blanch peaches, place them in a saucepan of boiling water and boil for 30 to 45 seconds. Using a slotted spoon, transfer peaches to an ice-water bath. Now you will be able to easily remove the skins with a sharp knife.

¼ cup	unsweetened almond milk	60 mL
2 tsp	liquid honey	10 mL
½ tsp	ground flax seeds (flaxseed meal)	2 mL
¾ cup	frozen raspberries	175 mL
¾ cup	frozen sliced peaches	175 mL
	Ice cubes (optional)	

SUGGESTED TOPPINGS

Raspberries

Sliced or chopped peaches

Chopped almonds

Ground flax seeds (flaxseed meal)

1. In blender, combine almond milk, honey, flax seeds, raspberries and peaches. Secure lid and blend (from low to high if using a variable-speed blender) until smooth. If a thicker consistency is desired, add ice, one cube at a time, and blend until smooth.

2. Pour into a bowl and top with any of the suggested toppings, as desired.

Variation

Substitute your favorite milk for the almond milk in this recipe.

Creamy Strawberry Smoothie Bowl

This smoothie bowl is delectably creamy thanks to the vanilla Greek yogurt and frozen banana.

Tip

Be sure to check the date on your yogurt before purchasing it. It should not be past the "sell by" or "best before" date on the container.

¾ cup	vanilla-flavored Greek yogurt	175 mL
¼ cup	unsweetened almond milk	60 mL
1	frozen banana, cut into pieces if necessary (see page 14)	1
½ cup	frozen strawberries	125 mL
	Ice cubes (optional)	

SUGGESTED TOPPINGS

Sliced strawberries
Sliced banana
Chopped pecans
Chia seeds

1. In blender, combine yogurt, almond milk, banana and strawberries. Secure lid and blend (from low to high if using a variable-speed blender) until smooth. If a thicker consistency is desired, add ice, one cube at a time, and blend until smooth.

2. Pour into a bowl and top with any of the suggested toppings, as desired.

Strawberry Mango Kefir Smoothie Bowl

Kefir is similar to drinkable yogurt. It's a healthy, creamy liquid addition to smoothie bowls, such as this fabulous one.

○◇○

**MAKES
1 SERVING**

Tips

If you use frozen strawberries, you will not need to add any ice.

If you prefer, you can use store-bought granola or any of the other granola recipes in this book (pages 210–218) to top your smoothie bowl.

¼ cup	strawberry-flavored kefir	60 mL
1 tsp	liquid honey	5 mL
1	frozen banana, cut into pieces if necessary (see page 14)	1
1 cup	frozen chopped mango	250 mL
¾ cup	strawberries	175 mL
	Ice cubes (optional)	

SUGGESTED TOPPINGS

Sliced strawberries

Sliced banana

Maple Cinnamon Granola (page 211)

Chia seeds

1. In blender, combine kefir, honey, banana, mango and strawberries. Secure lid and blend (from low to high if using a variable-speed blender) until smooth. If a thicker consistency is desired, add ice, one cube at a time, and blend until smooth.

2. Pour into a bowl and top with any of the suggested toppings, as desired.

Triple-Berry Oat Bowl

If you are looking for an immune-boosting, illness-busting recipe, this one has all the right ingredients.

○-○○-○

**MAKES
1 SERVING**

Tip

Store ground flax seeds in an airtight plastic bag in the refrigerator or freezer.

¼ cup	unsweetened almond milk	60 mL
¼ cup	large-flake (old-fashioned) rolled oats	60 mL
2 tsp	ground flax seeds (flaxseed meal)	10 mL
½ cup	frozen strawberries	125 mL
½ cup	frozen blueberries	125 mL
1 cup	blackberries	250 mL
	Ice cubes (optional)	

SUGGESTED TOPPINGS

Sliced strawberries

Blackberries

Blueberries

Rolled oats

Ground flax seeds (flaxseed meal)

1. In blender, combine almond milk, oats, flax seeds, strawberries, blueberries and blackberries. Secure lid and blend (from low to high if using a variable-speed blender) until smooth. If a thicker consistency is desired, add ice, one cube at a time, and blend until smooth.

2. Pour into a bowl and top with any of the suggested toppings, as desired.

Variation

Add 1 tbsp (15 mL) protein powder for additional protein and thickness. Blend it with the almond milk before adding the remaining ingredients.

Cherry Berry Chia Bowl

Love cherries but rue their short season? This smoothie bowl allows you to enjoy them all year long!

Tip

When purchasing coconut water, be sure to read labels. Avoid coconut water from concentrate and any that has additives, sweeteners or unusual ingredients.

¼ cup	unsweetened coconut milk beverage or water	60 mL
1 tsp	liquid honey	5 mL
½ tsp	chia seeds	2 mL
1 cup	frozen pitted cherries	250 mL
1 cup	mixed berries	250 mL
1	ripe banana	1
	Ice cubes (optional)	

SUGGESTED TOPPINGS

Berries

Sliced banana

Pitted cherries

Sesame seeds

Chia seeds

1. In blender, combine coconut milk, honey, chia seeds, cherries, berries and banana. Secure lid and blend (from low to high if using a variable-speed blender) until smooth. If a thicker consistency is desired, add ice, one cube at a time, and blend until smooth.

2. Pour into a bowl and top with any of the suggested toppings, as desired.

Cherry Oat Bowl

Cherries are nutritional superstars. One cup (250 mL) of raw cherries has 87 calories, 22 grams of carbohydrates, 1 gram of protein and 3 grams of fiber. Enjoy them during the summertime while they are at their peak or use frozen pitted cherries.

MAKES 2 SERVINGS

Tip

When pitting cherries, wear an apron or an old T-shirt — it's messy work! Use a cherry pitter and work over a large bowl or the sink. Make sure to double-check the cherries before adding them to the blender, in case you missed any pits.

½ cup	vanilla-flavored Greek yogurt	125 mL
¼ cup	steel-cut oats	60 mL
1 tsp	ground flax seeds (flaxseed meal)	5 mL
½	frozen banana, cut into pieces if necessary (see page 14)	½
1 cup	cherries, pitted (fresh or frozen)	250 mL
¼ cup	blackberries (fresh or frozen)	60 mL
	Ice cubes (optional)	

SUGGESTED TOPPINGS

Cherries

Sliced banana

Blackberries

Rolled oats

Cherry Almond Granola (page 215)

Chopped nuts

Ground flax seeds (flaxseed meal)

1. In blender, combine yogurt, oats, flax seeds, banana, cherries and blackberries. Secure lid and blend (from low to high if using a variable-speed blender) until smooth. If a thicker consistency is desired, add ice, one cube at a time, and blend until smooth.

2. Pour into bowls and top with any of the suggested toppings, as desired.

Variation

Large-flake (old-fashioned) rolled oats may be substituted for the steel-cut oats.

Fig Berry Smoothie Bowl

Figs are very high in fiber and are a great source of minerals.

**MAKES
1 SERVING**

Tip

Fresh figs have a very short peak season and a short shelf life. To freeze leftover ripe figs, wash them thoroughly, spread them out on a baking sheet and freeze. When frozen solid, transfer to freezer bags and store in the freezer for up to 6 months.

½ cup	unsweetened almond milk	125 mL
1 tbsp	protein powder	15 mL
1	frozen banana, cut into pieces if necessary (see page 14)	1
1 cup	frozen strawberries	250 mL
3	fresh or dried figs, stems removed	3
	Ice cubes	

SUGGESTED TOPPINGS

Blueberries

Strawberries

Chopped trimmed dried figs

Kitchen Sink Granola (page 218)

1. In blender, combine almond milk and protein powder. Secure lid and blend (from low to high if using a variable-speed blender) until smooth. Add banana, strawberries and figs; blend until smooth. Add ice, one cube at a time, blending until the desired consistency is achieved.

2. Pour into a bowl and top with any of the suggested toppings, as desired.

Date Almond Butter Bowl

Dates paired with almond butter, almond milk and cacao powder create a filling breakfast, afternoon snack or dessert.

MAKES 1 SERVING

Tips

Purchase pitted dates where dried fruits are sold in your local grocery store. Use leftover dates in baked goods or protein ball recipes, or in smoothies as a fiber-filled sweetener.

If you don't have a high-powered blender, finely chop the dates, then soak them in the almond milk for 15 to 20 minutes or until the dates begin to plump. Add the dates and almond milk to the blender and continue with the recipe.

If you prefer, you can use store-bought almond butter in place of homemade.

¼ cup	unsweetened almond milk	60 mL
2 tsp	unsweetened cocoa powder	10 mL
1	frozen banana, cut into pieces if necessary (see page 14)	1
½ cup	pitted dates (see tips, at left)	125 mL
2 tbsp	Homemade Almond Butter (page 226)	30 mL
	Ice cubes	

SUGGESTED TOPPINGS

Unsweetened cocoa powder
Unsweetened shredded coconut
Chopped pecans
Chopped almonds
Mini chocolate chips

1. In blender, combine almond milk, cocoa, banana, dates and almond butter. Secure lid and blend (from low to high if using a variable-speed blender) until smooth. Add ice, one cube at a time, blending until the desired consistency is achieved.

2. Pour into a bowl and top with any of the suggested toppings, as desired.

Pear Pleaser

This is a great way to use up overripe pears. I like to use Bartlett pears for this smoothie bowl, but any variety will work, so choose your favorite!

**MAKES
1 SERVING**

Tip

Make sure your pear is ripe and sweet. There's no need to peel the pear before blending.

¼ cup	unsweetened almond milk	60 mL
2 tsp	vanilla extract	10 mL
1	frozen banana, cut into pieces if necessary (see page 14)	1
1	ripe pear, sliced	1
4	ice cubes	4

SUGGESTED TOPPINGS

Sliced pear

Sliced banana

Chia seeds

Ground flax seeds (flaxseed meal)

Hemp seeds

1. In blender, combine almond milk, vanilla, banana, pear and ice. Secure lid and blend (from low to high if using a variable-speed blender) until smooth.

2. Pour into a bowl and top with any of the suggested toppings, as desired.

Variations

Add 1 tbsp (15 mL) protein powder for additional thickness and protein. Blend it with the liquids before adding the remaining ingredients.

For an even sweeter smoothie bowl, add 1 tsp (5 mL) liquid honey with the liquids.

Apricot Berry Bowl

My kids love apricots, and when I paired them with raspberries, this smoothie bowl was a huge breakfast hit.

MAKES 1 SERVING

Tips

Fresh apricots can typically be found in stores from May through August. Add them to cereal or serve them in a salad or alongside pork, chicken, pancakes or waffles.

Look for apricot nectar in the juice section of the grocery store.

¼ cup	apricot nectar	60 mL
¾ cup	frozen raspberries	175 mL
½ cup	halved fresh or dried apricots	125 mL
	Ice cubes	

SUGGESTED TOPPINGS

Chopped dried apricots

Raspberries

Easy Muesli (page 219)

Ground flax seeds (flaxseed meal)

1. In blender, combine apricot nectar, raspberries and apricots. Secure lid and blend (from low to high if using a variable-speed blender) until smooth. Add ice, one cube at a time, blending until the desired consistency is achieved.

2. Pour into a bowl and top with any of the suggested toppings, as desired.

Variation

Substitute unsweetened orange juice, apple juice or coconut water for the apricot nectar.

Nectarine Banana Bowl

Nutmeg brings out the nectarines' flavor in this delectable smoothie bowl.

**MAKES
2 SERVINGS**

Tip

Store nectarines and peaches at room temperature until ripe, which can take 2 to 3 days. To speed up the ripening process, place them in a paper bag. Be sure to keep them out of direct sunlight.

⅓ cup	milk	75 mL
½	scoop protein powder	½
½ tsp	ground nutmeg	2 mL
1	frozen banana, cut into pieces if necessary (see page 14)	1
2	ripe nectarines, sliced	2
4	ice cubes	4

SUGGESTED TOPPINGS

Ground nutmeg or cinnamon

Sliced nectarine

Sliced banana

Maple Cinnamon Granola (page 211)

1. In blender, combine milk and protein powder. Secure lid and blend (from low to high if using a variable-speed blender) until smooth. Add nutmeg, banana, nectarines and ice; blend until smooth.

2. Pour into bowls and top with any of the suggested toppings, as desired.

Variation

Peach Banana Bowl: Substitute 2 ripe peaches for the nectarines and replace the milk with ½ cup (125 mL) vanilla-flavored yogurt.

Healthy Peach Blueberry Bowl

Bananas don't just add smooth, creamy texture to smoothies, they also add potassium, which can help prevent leg and foot cramps.

Tip

Look for kefir in the dairy section of the grocery store.

⅓ cup	blueberry- or vanilla-flavored kefir	75 mL
1 tbsp	protein powder	15 mL
1	frozen banana, cut into pieces if necessary (see page 14)	1
½ cup	frozen sliced peaches	125 mL
1 cup	blueberries (fresh or frozen)	250 mL
	Ice cubes	

SUGGESTED TOPPINGS

Blueberries

Sliced peaches

Sliced banana

Chia seeds

1. In blender, combine kefir and protein powder. Secure lid and blend (from low to high if using a variable-speed blender) until smooth. Add banana, peaches and blueberries; blend until smooth. Add ice, one cube at a time, blending until the desired consistency is achieved.

2. Pour into a bowl and top with any of the suggested toppings, as desired.

Plum Honeydew Bowl

This smoothie is packed with vitamin C from the plums, honeydew and grapes. For best flavor, make sure your fruit is ripe and at its peak season.

MAKES 1 TO 2 SERVINGS

Tip

If you're having a busy week, purchase honeydew that is already cut into chunks to make this recipe faster and easier.

3 tbsp	coconut water	45 mL
2 tsp	liquid honey	10 mL
1 tbsp	unsweetened shredded coconut	15 mL
1 tbsp	large-flake (old-fashioned) rolled oats	15 mL
¼ cup	frozen green grapes	60 mL
2	plums, chopped (about 1 cup/250 mL)	2
¾ cup	chopped honeydew melon	175 mL
	Ice cubes (optional)	

SUGGESTED TOPPINGS

Ground cinnamon
Sliced plums
Unsweetened shredded coconut
Cherry Almond Granola (page 215)

1. In blender, combine coconut water, honey, coconut, oats, grapes, plums and melon. Secure lid and blend (from low to high if using a variable-speed blender) until smooth. If a thicker consistency is desired, add ice, one cube at a time, and blend until smooth.

2. Pour into a bowl or bowls and top with any of the suggested toppings, as desired.

Watermelon Pomegranate Bowl

The colors of this smoothie are so rich you can almost see the health benefits. It's perfect after a summer workout.

Tips

Look for pomegranate juice in the refrigerated section of the produce department (not in the non-refrigerated juice section).

Use leftover pomegranate juice as a splash to flavor your water.

¼ cup	unsweetened pomegranate juice	60 mL
½	frozen banana, cut into pieces if necessary (see page 14)	½
½ cup	frozen mango chunks	125 mL
1½ cups	chopped watermelon	375 mL
	Ice cubes (optional)	

SUGGESTED TOPPINGS

Sliced banana

Chopped watermelon

Pomegranate seeds

Classic Granola (page 210)

1. In blender, combine pomegranate juice, banana, mango and watermelon. Secure lid and blend (from low to high if using a variable-speed blender) until smooth. If a thicker consistency is desired, add ice, one cube at a time, and blend until smooth.

2. Pour into a bowl and top with any of the suggested toppings, as desired.

Go Grapefruit

Consuming grapefruit is said to curb your hunger. I love it in this breakfast smoothie bowl.

MAKES 1 SERVING

Tip

A ripe grapefruit will have a bright color and should feel heavier than it looks.

¼ cup	freshly squeezed red grapefruit juice	60 mL
1 tsp	liquid honey	5 mL
½	frozen banana, cut into pieces if necessary (see page 14)	½
½ cup	frozen strawberries	125 mL
1 cup	sliced red grapefruit	250 mL
	Ice cubes (optional)	

SUGGESTED TOPPINGS

Sliced strawberries

Sliced grapefruit

Blueberries

Sliced banana

Classic Granola (page 210)

1. In blender, combine grapefruit juice, honey, banana, strawberries and grapefruit. Secure lid and blend (from low to high if using a variable-speed blender) until smooth. If a thicker consistency is desired, add ice, one cube at a time, and blend until smooth.

2. Pour into a bowl and top with any of the suggested toppings, as desired.

Wake-Up Orange Bowl

Frozen fruit is just as nutritious as fresh. It is picked at its peak and flash frozen, so it retains all of its vitamins and minerals. Use any of your favorite frozen mixed fruit in this recipe.

○○

MAKES 2 SERVINGS

Tip

Purchase frozen mixed fruit to use in a variety of smoothie bowl recipes. It's typically chopped or sliced before it's frozen, so you'll save on prep time.

½ cup	freshly squeezed orange juice	125 mL
1	scoop protein powder	1
½	frozen banana, cut into pieces if necessary (see page 14)	½
1 cup	frozen mixed fruit	250 mL
	Ice cubes	

SUGGESTED TOPPINGS

Raspberries

Blueberries

Sliced banana

Classic Granola (page 210)

1. In blender, combine orange juice and protein powder. Secure lid and blend (from low to high if using a variable-speed blender) until smooth. Add banana and mixed fruit; blend until smooth. Add ice, one cube at a time, blending until the desired consistency is achieved.

2. Pour into bowls and top with any of the suggested toppings, as desired.

Mandarin Orange Refuel

This is my husband's go-to smoothie bowl recipe after a morning workout.

⅓ cup	freshly squeezed orange juice	75 mL
1	scoop protein powder	1
1	frozen banana, cut into pieces if necessary (see page 14)	1
1½ cups	frozen mixed chopped mango, mandarin oranges, bananas, pineapple and sweet potatoes (see tip, at left)	375 mL
	Ice cubes (optional)	

SUGGESTED TOPPINGS

Sliced banana

Chopped oranges

Dried pineapple pieces

Granola

Ground flax seeds (flaxseed meal)

**MAKES
1 SERVING**

Tips

Look for packages of frozen mixed fruit and vegetables, such as Dole Fruit & Veggie Orange Medley, in the freezer section of your grocery store. If you cannot find a packaged mix, use ½ cup (125 mL) each frozen chopped mango, pineapple and oranges.

You can use store-bought granola or any of the granola recipes in this book (pages 210–218) to top your smoothie bowl.

1. In blender, combine orange juice and protein powder. Secure lid and blend (from low to high if using a variable-speed blender) until smooth. Add banana and mixed fruits and vegetables; blend until smooth. If a thicker consistency is desired, add ice, one cube at a time, and blend until smooth.

2. Pour into a bowl and top with any of the suggested toppings, as desired.

Sunrise Smoothie Bowl

"Delicious, refreshing and filling!" is what my husband said when he tasted this one. It's all of those, and beautiful, too!

MAKES 1 TO 2 SERVINGS

Tips

Prepare homemade granola (see recipes, pages 210–218) as often as possible. If you're short on time and need to use store-bought granola, be sure to read the ingredient list and choose one that is low in sugar and has no added artificial ingredients.

Omit the granola in the smoothie if you don't like the crunchy texture, and add more in the topping.

1 cup	plain Greek yogurt	250 mL
¼ cup	freshly squeezed orange juice	60 mL
2 tbsp	Classic Granola (page 210)	30 mL
½ tsp	ground flax seeds (flaxseed meal)	2 mL
1	frozen banana, cut into pieces if necessary (see page 14)	1
1 cup	sliced oranges	250 mL
	Ice cubes (optional)	

SUGGESTED TOPPINGS

Sliced banana

Sliced orange

Classic Granola

Ground flax seeds (flaxseed meal)

1. In blender, combine yogurt, orange juice, granola, flax seeds, banana and oranges. Secure lid and blend (from low to high if using a variable-speed blender) until smooth. If a thicker consistency is desired, add ice, one cube at a time, and blend until smooth.

2. Pour into a bowl or bowls and top with any of the suggested toppings, as desired.

Three-Ingredient Coco-Pineapple

Full of vitamin C, versatile pineapple is one of my favorite smoothie bowl ingredients. It can be added to almost any fruit smoothie bowl.

MAKES 1 SERVING

Tips

To save money, purchase a whole fresh pineapple to cut into chunks and freeze. Cutting up a pineapple is easy. Lay it down on a cutting board and trim about 1 inch (2.5 cm) off the bottom and top. Stand it upright and slice off the sides, including the dark spots (often called "eyes"). Lay it down again and quarter it lengthwise. Cut out the hard core and cut pineapple into chunks.

Toast coconut in a preheated 350°F (180°C) oven for 6 to 8 minutes (or under the broiler for 2 minutes), until lightly browned.

⅓ cup	unsweetened coconut milk beverage	75 mL
1	frozen banana, cut into pieces if necessary (see page 14)	1
1 cup	frozen pineapple chunks	250 mL
	Ice cubes (optional)	

SUGGESTED TOPPINGS

Sliced banana

Chopped pineapple

Toasted unsweetened shredded coconut (see tip, at left)

Coconut Granola (page 216)

Chopped nuts

1. In blender, combine coconut milk, banana and pineapple. Secure lid and blend (from low to high if using a variable-speed blender) until smooth. If a thicker consistency is desired, add ice, one cube at a time, and blend until smooth.

2. Pour into a bowl and top with any of the suggested toppings, as desired.

Variation

Add 1 scoop of protein powder for additional protein and thickness. Blend it with the coconut milk before adding the remaining ingredients.

Kiwi Kick-Start

My three children are huge kiwi fans! One kiwi has 45 calories, 10 grams of carbohydrate, less than 0.5 grams of fat and 2 grams of fiber.

MAKES 1 SERVING

Tips

Kiwis also make a tasty addition to salads, or they're great over yogurt or just on their own. Peel and slice them ahead so you can eat them anytime. Store sliced kiwi in an airtight container in the refrigerator for up to 2 days.

If you prefer, you can use store-bought banana chips to top your smoothie bowl.

½ cup	coconut water	125 mL
1 tbsp	liquid honey	15 mL
1	frozen banana, cut into pieces if necessary (see page 14)	1
½ cup	frozen sliced peaches	125 mL
3	kiwifruit, peeled	3
	Ice cubes (optional)	

SUGGESTED TOPPINGS

Sliced kiwifruit
Sliced banana
Unsweetened coconut flakes
Banana Chips (page 208)
Ground flax seeds (flaxseed meal)

1. In blender, combine coconut water, honey, banana, peaches and kiwis. Secure lid and blend (from low to high if using a variable-speed blender) until smooth. If a thicker consistency is desired, add ice, one cube at a time, and blend until smooth.

2. Pour into a bowl and top with any of the suggested toppings, as desired.

Papaya Coconut Bowl

This recipe is a great way to start enjoying papaya if you're unfamiliar with it. It's so good for breakfast, after a workout or after school.

○⊂○⊃○⊂○⊃○⊂○⊃○⊂○⊃○⊂○⊃○⊂○⊃○⊂○⊃○⊂○⊃○⊂○⊃○⊂○⊃○⊂○⊃○⊂○⊃○⊂○⊃○⊂○⊃○⊂○⊃○⊂○⊃

MAKES 1 SERVING

Tip

Look for frozen papaya chunks in the frozen fruit section of the grocery store.

⅓ cup	coconut water	75 mL
1 tsp	liquid honey	5 mL
1 tbsp	unsweetened shredded coconut	15 mL
½	frozen banana, cut into pieces if necessary (see page 14)	½
1½ cups	frozen papaya chunks	375 mL
	Ice cubes (optional)	

SUGGESTED TOPPINGS

Sliced banana

Blueberries

Unsweetened shredded coconut

Coconut Granola (page 216)

Green pumpkin seeds (pepitas)

1. In blender, combine coconut water, honey, coconut, banana and papaya. Secure lid and blend (from low to high if using a variable-speed blender) until smooth. If a thicker consistency is desired, add ice, one cube at a time, and blend until smooth.

2. Pour into a bowl and top with any of the suggested toppings, as desired.

Variation

Add 1 scoop of protein powder for additional protein and thickness. Blend it with the liquids before adding the remaining ingredients.

Green Creations

Clean Green Bowl

A general healthy guideline is to eat at least five servings of fruits and vegetables daily. You're off to a great start with this smoothie bowl.

MAKES 2 SERVINGS

Tip

Frozen grapes are a great choice for smoothie bowls because they add thickness and enable you to use less ice.

¼ cup	coconut water	60 mL
1	frozen banana, cut into pieces if necessary (see page 14)	1
¼ cup	frozen green grapes	60 mL
2 cups	trimmed baby spinach leaves	500 mL
1 cup	chopped romaine lettuce	250 mL
½ cup	chopped celery	125 mL
2 tbsp	fresh cilantro leaves (optional)	30 mL
1 tsp	grated lemon zest	5 mL
	Ice cubes (optional)	

SUGGESTED TOPPINGS

Sliced banana

Sliced green grapes

Unsweetened shredded coconut

Chopped pecans

Hemp seeds

Ground flax seeds (flaxseed meal)

1. In blender, combine coconut water, banana, grapes, spinach, romaine, celery, cilantro (if using) and lemon zest. Secure lid and blend (from low to high if using a variable-speed blender) until smooth. If a thicker consistency is desired, add ice, one cube at a time, and blend until smooth.

2. Pour into bowls and top with any of the suggested toppings, as desired.

Variation

Substitute unsweetened apple juice for the coconut water.

Superfood Smoothie Bowl

With all these fabulous superfoods, this tastes like health in a bowl.

MAKES 2 SERVINGS

Tip

If you use frozen raspberries, you may not need any ice.

¼ cup	water	60 mL
2 tsp	liquid honey	10 mL
1	frozen banana, cut into pieces if necessary (see page 14)	1
1 cup	pineapple chunks (fresh or frozen)	250 mL
1 cup	trimmed baby spinach leaves	250 mL
½ cup	raspberries (fresh or frozen)	125 mL
½ cup	chopped celery	125 mL
	Ice cubes (optional)	

SUGGESTED TOPPINGS

Sliced banana

Chopped pineapple

Raspberries

Kitchen Sink Granola (page 218)

Ground flax seeds (flaxseed meal)

1. In blender, combine water, honey, banana, pineapple and spinach. Secure lid and blend (from low to high if using a variable-speed blender) until smooth. Add raspberries and celery; blend until smooth. If a thicker consistency is desired, add ice, one cube at a time, and blend until smooth.

2. Pour into bowls and top with any of the suggested toppings, as desired.

Chocolate Superfood Bowl

This recipe is filled with superfoods (super-healthy ingredients), including blueberries, avocado and cocoa powder.

Tip

Refrigerate blueberries for up to 1 week. Wash only before using them.

¼ cup	unsweetened almond milk	60 mL
2 tsp	liquid honey	10 mL
1 tsp	natural unsweetened cocoa powder (not Dutch process)	5 mL
1	frozen banana, cut into pieces if necessary (see page 14)	1
½	avocado	½
3 tbsp	blueberries	45 mL
4	ice cubes	4

SUGGESTED TOPPINGS

Natural unsweetened cocoa powder

Sliced banana

Blueberries

Unsweetened flaked coconut

No-Bake Flaxseed Bars (page 222), crumbled

Chia seeds

1. In blender, combine almond milk, honey, cocoa, banana and avocado. Secure lid and blend (from low to high if using a variable-speed blender) until smooth. Add blueberries and ice; blend until smooth.

2. Pour into a bowl and top with any of the suggested toppings, as desired.

Spinach Almond Bowl

My kids said this smoothie bowl sounded "scary," but then they ate it all up.

Tips

Store spinach leaves loosely wrapped in paper towels and tightly sealed in a plastic bag in the refrigerator for up to 3 days.

If you prefer, you can use store-bought almond butter in place of homemade.

1 cup	coconut water	250 mL
1 tsp	vanilla extract	5 mL
1	frozen banana, cut into pieces if necessary (see page 14)	1
2 cups	trimmed spinach leaves	500 mL
2 tbsp	Homemade Almond Butter (page 226)	30 mL
	Ice cubes (optional)	

SUGGESTED TOPPINGS

Sliced banana

Unsweetened shredded coconut

Easy Muesli (page 219)

Cherry Almond Granola (page 215)

1. In blender, combine coconut water, vanilla, banana, spinach and almond butter. Secure lid and blend (from low to high if using a variable-speed blender) until smooth. If a thicker consistency is desired, add ice, one cube at a time, and blend until smooth.

2. Pour into a bowl and top with any of the suggested toppings, as desired.

Blackberry Coconut Bowl

If you're under the weather, this recipe may just help you feel better.

Tip

If you use fresh blackberries instead of frozen, you will only need ¼ cup (60 mL) coconut milk, and you will need 4 ice cubes.

⅓ cup	unsweetened coconut milk beverage	75 mL
½	frozen banana, cut into pieces if necessary (see page 14)	½
½ cup	frozen blackberries	125 mL
1½ cups	trimmed baby spinach leaves	375 mL
	Ice cubes	

SUGGESTED TOPPINGS

Sliced banana

Blackberries

Coconut Granola (page 216)

Green pumpkin seeds (pepitas)

1. In blender, combine coconut milk, banana, blackberries and spinach. Secure lid and blend (from low to high if using a variable-speed blender) until smooth. Add ice, one cube at a time, blending until the desired consistency is achieved.

2. Pour into a bowl and top with any of the suggested toppings, as desired.

Blueberry Flaxseed Bowl

Flax seeds are a great source of omega-3 fatty acids and fiber, and no one will know you added them to this recipe. Flax seeds can be added to any smoothie bowl, sprinkled on top of cereals or added to baked goods.

○◇○

**MAKES
1 SERVING**

Tip

This recipe can be prepared with any type of berries. Use a berry-flavored yogurt to match the type of berries you are using.

½ cup	blueberry-flavored yogurt	125 mL
¼ cup	unsweetened apple juice	60 mL
1 tsp	ground flax seeds (flaxseed meal)	5 mL
1	frozen banana, cut into pieces if necessary (see page 14)	1
1 cup	blueberries (fresh or frozen)	250 mL
2 cups	trimmed baby spinach leaves or arugula	500 mL
	Ice cubes (optional)	

SUGGESTED TOPPINGS

Sliced banana

Blueberries

Classic Granola (page 210)

Ground flax seeds (flaxseed meal)

1. In blender, combine yogurt, apple juice, flax seeds, banana, blueberries and spinach. Secure lid and blend (from low to high if using a variable-speed blender) until smooth. If a thicker consistency is desired, add ice, one cube at a time, and blend until smooth.

2. Pour into a bowl and top with any of the suggested toppings, as desired.

Berry Green Bowl

The oats in this recipe add thickness to your smoothie bowl. If you prefer, you can feel free to substitute 1 scoop of protein powder.

**MAKES
1 SERVING**

Tips

If you use sweetened almond milk instead of unsweetened, omit the honey.

If you use frozen berries, you will not need to add any ice.

If you're following a gluten-free diet, purchase certified gluten-free oats.

¼ cup	unsweetened almond milk	60 mL
1 tbsp	liquid honey	15 mL
2 tbsp	large-flake (old-fashioned) rolled oats	30 mL
½ cup	blackberries (fresh or frozen)	125 mL
½ cup	strawberries (fresh or frozen)	125 mL
1½ cups	trimmed baby spinach leaves	375 mL
	Ice cubes (optional)	

SUGGESTED TOPPINGS

Blackberries

Sliced strawberries

Classic Granola (page 210)

Large-flake (old-fashioned) rolled oats

Green pumpkin seeds (pepitas)

1. In blender, combine almond milk, honey, oats, blackberries, strawberries and spinach. Secure lid and blend (from low to high if using a variable-speed blender) until smooth. If a thicker consistency is desired, add ice, one cube at a time, and blend until smooth.

2. Pour into a bowl and top with any of the suggested toppings, as desired.

Raspberry Mint Bowl

Raspberries and mint are a terrific combination. Add spinach, banana, lime and honey and you get one amazing smoothie bowl.

**MAKES
2 SERVINGS**

Tip

If you prefer, you can use store-bought granola to top your smoothie bowl.

¼ cup	water	60 mL
2 tbsp	freshly squeezed lime juice	30 mL
1 tbsp	liquid honey	15 mL
1	frozen banana, cut into pieces if necessary (see page 14)	1
1 cup	raspberries (fresh or frozen)	250 mL
1 cup	trimmed baby spinach leaves	250 mL
2 tbsp	fresh mint leaves	30 mL
	Ice cubes (optional)	

SUGGESTED TOPPINGS

Sliced banana

Classic Granola (page 210)

Sunflower seeds

Fresh mint leaves

1. In blender, combine water, lime juice, honey, banana, raspberries, spinach and mint. Secure lid and blend (from low to high if using a variable-speed blender) until smooth. If a thicker consistency is desired, add ice, one cube at a time, and blend until smooth.

2. Pour into bowls and top with any of the suggested toppings, as desired.

Variations

For added flavor, substitute ¼ cup (60 mL) coconut water for the water.

Substitute 1 cup (250 mL) frozen strawberries or chopped cantaloupe for the raspberries.

Strawberry Avocado Bowl

I make this smoothie bowl often, not telling my kids that it contains avocado. It makes a great breakfast before school or work.

	MAKES 2 SERVINGS		

Tips

If you use frozen strawberries, you will not need to add ice.

Any type of milk — dairy or nondairy — can be substituted for the almond milk.

To slice an avocado, use a sharp knife to cut lengthwise around the pit. Twist to open, and discard the pit. Cut around the edges and lift avocado flesh out.

¼ cup	unsweetened almond milk	60 mL
1 tsp	liquid honey	5 mL
½	frozen banana, cut into pieces if necessary (see page 14)	½
¾ cup	frozen pineapple chunks	175 mL
1 cup	hulled strawberries (fresh or frozen)	250 mL
½	avocado	½
1 tsp	chia seeds	5 mL
	Ice cubes (optional)	

SUGGESTED TOPPINGS
Sliced banana
Sliced strawberries
Healthy Trail Mix (page 220)
Chia seeds

1. In blender, combine almond milk, honey, banana, pineapple and strawberries. Secure lid and blend (from low to high if using a variable-speed blender) until smooth. Add avocado and chia seeds; blend until smooth. If a thicker consistency is desired, add ice, one cube at a time, and blend until smooth.

2. Pour into bowls and top with any of the suggested toppings, as desired.

Three-Berry Smoothie Bowl

Three types of berries, kale and banana work together to create a nutritious, tasty smoothie bowl.

MAKES 1 SERVING

Tips

You may substitute ¾ cup (175 mL) mixed frozen berries for the raspberries, blackberries and blueberries. If you use frozen berries, you may not need to use any ice. Add ice, one cube at a time, blending until the desired consistency is achieved.

Coconut water can be substituted for the coconut milk.

If you prefer, you can use store-bought banana chips to top your smoothie bowl.

⅓ cup	unsweetened coconut milk beverage	75 mL
½	frozen banana, cut into pieces if necessary (see page 14)	½
1½ cups	trimmed kale leaves	375 mL
¼ cup	raspberries	60 mL
¼ cup	blackberries	60 mL
¼ cup	blueberries	60 mL
4	ice cubes (see tip, at left)	4

SUGGESTED TOPPINGS

Goji berries

Sliced strawberries

Blueberries

Unsweetened shredded coconut

Banana Chips (page 208)

1. In blender, combine coconut milk, banana, kale, raspberries, blackberries, blueberries and ice. Secure lid and blend (from low to high if using a variable-speed blender) until smooth.

2. Pour into a bowl and top with any of the suggested toppings, as desired.

Cherry Kale Bowl

If cherries are not in season, feel free to use frozen. They are picked at their peak and flash-frozen, so they will be just as sweet.

◇◇

Tip

Store overripe bananas in the freezer for smoothie bowls. You can often find overripe bananas on sale at the grocery store, so stock up on them.

¼ cup	coconut water	60 mL
½	frozen banana, cut into pieces if necessary (see page 14)	½
1 cup	pitted cherries (fresh or frozen)	250 mL
¾ cup	trimmed kale leaves	175 mL
4	ice cubes	4

SUGGESTED TOPPINGS

Sliced banana

Pitted cherries

Unsweetened shredded coconut

Cherry Almond Granola (page 215)

1. In blender, combine coconut water, banana, cherries, kale and ice. Secure lid and blend (from low to high if using a variable-speed blender) until smooth.

2. Pour into a bowl and top with any of the suggested toppings, as desired.

Energy Booster

The combination of cherries, spinach and fresh pear creates this nutritional powerhouse of a smoothie bowl that will help boost your energy levels.

Tip

Choose pears that smell fragrant. They shouldn't be as solid as a rock, but they shouldn't be too soft, either.

⅓ cup	unsweetened almond milk	75 mL
½	frozen banana, cut into pieces if necessary (see page 14)	½
¾ cup	frozen pitted cherries	175 mL
1	Bartlett pear, sliced	1
1 cup	trimmed baby spinach leaves	250 mL
	Ice cubes (optional)	

SUGGESTED TOPPINGS

Sliced banana

Sliced pear

Kitchen Sink Granola (page 218)

Chia seeds

1. In blender, combine almond milk, banana, cherries, pear and spinach. Secure lid and blend (from low to high if using a variable-speed blender) until smooth. If a thicker consistency is desired, add ice, one cube at a time, and blend until smooth.

2. Pour into a bowl or bowls and top with any of the suggested toppings, as desired.

Ginger Pear Bowl

Treat yourself to this easy green smoothie that packs plenty of nutrition with grapes, ginger, spinach and pear.

Tips

Frozen grapes are great for this recipe and other smoothie bowls. To freeze, wash grapes thoroughly and blot dry with a paper towel. Place them in a single layer on a baking sheet in the freezer. When solid, transfer to a freezer bag, seal and keep frozen for up to 3 months.

If you prefer, you can use store-bought granola to top your smoothie bowl.

¼ cup	coconut water	60 mL
½ cup	frozen red grapes	125 mL
1	pear, sliced	1
1 cup	trimmed baby spinach leaves	250 mL
1 tsp	grated gingerroot	5 mL
4	ice cubes	4

SUGGESTED TOPPINGS

Sliced red grapes
Sliced pear
Unsweetened shredded coconut
Kitchen Sink Granola (page 218)

1. In blender, combine coconut water, grapes, pear, spinach, ginger and ice. Secure lid and blend (from low to high if using a variable-speed blender) until smooth.

2. Pour into a bowl and top with any of the suggested toppings, as desired.

Kale Pear Bowl

This smoothie bowl will give you energy and plenty of vitamins, so eat up!

Tip

If you prefer, you can use store-bought granola to top your smoothie bowl.

¼ cup	unsweetened almond milk	60 mL
½	frozen banana, cut into pieces if necessary (see page 14)	½
⅓ cup	frozen green grapes	75 mL
1	Bartlett pear, sliced	1
1 cup	trimmed kale leaves	250 mL
4	ice cubes	4

SUGGESTED TOPPINGS

Sliced banana

Sliced pear

Sliced green grapes

Kitchen Sink Granola (page 218)

Hemp seeds

1. In blender, combine almond milk, banana, grapes, pear, kale and ice. Secure lid and blend (from low to high if using a variable-speed blender) until smooth.

2. Pour into a bowl and top with any of the suggested toppings, as desired.

Parsley Pear Bowl

Pears are a good source of potassium and vitamins B_2, C and E. Make sure to use ripe pears to make your smoothie bowls.

MAKES 2 SERVINGS

Tips

If you can't find Bartlett pears, use Comice or Anjou pears.

You don't have to peel the pears before adding them to the blender, but you can if you prefer.

If you don't like parsley, feel free to omit it and use another herb instead.

If you prefer, you can use store-bought banana chips to top your smoothie bowl.

¼ cup	water	60 mL
1	frozen banana, cut into pieces if necessary (see page 14)	1
1 cup	frozen sliced peaches	250 mL
2	Bartlett pears, sliced	2
½	avocado	½
⅓ cup	fresh parsley leaves	75 mL
	Ice cubes (optional)	

SUGGESTED TOPPINGS

Sliced pear

Banana Chips (page 208)

Ground flax seeds (flaxseed meal)

1. In blender, combine water, banana, peaches, pears, avocado and parsley. Secure lid and blend (from low to high if using a variable-speed blender) until smooth. If a thicker consistency is desired, add ice, one cube at a time, and blend until smooth.

2. Pour into bowls and top with any of the suggested toppings, as desired.

Fig Grape Bowl

Fresh figs are readily available in the summertime, but imported fresh figs can often be found in fall and early winter, too. Figs are loaded with B vitamins, calcium and fiber, and even have 2 grams of protein.

MAKES 2 SERVINGS

Tip

Ripe figs are highly perishable. Use them as soon as possible after purchasing them.

¼ cup	water	60 mL
1 tsp	liquid honey	5 mL
½	frozen banana, cut into pieces if necessary (see page 14)	½
½ cup	frozen green grapes	125 mL
4	fresh or dried figs	4
2 cups	trimmed spinach leaves	500 mL
4	ice cubes	4

SUGGESTED TOPPINGS

Sliced banana

Chopped figs

Sliced green and red grapes

1. In blender, combine water, honey, banana and grapes. Secure lid and blend (from low to high if using a variable-speed blender) until smooth. Add figs, spinach and ice; blend until smooth.

2. Pour into bowls and top with any of the suggested toppings, as desired.

Peachy Green Bowl

One large peach contains just 68 calories and no fat. Add fresh spinach, banana and vanilla for a healthy green smoothie bowl.

Tip

You can use fresh peaches and an unfrozen ripe banana, but in that case add 4 additional cubes of ice, one at a time, blending until the desired consistency is achieved.

¼ cup	water	60 mL
1 tsp	vanilla extract	5 mL
1	scoop vanilla-flavored protein powder	1
½	frozen banana, cut into pieces if necessary (see page 14)	½
1 cup	frozen sliced peaches	250 mL
1½ cups	trimmed spinach leaves	375 mL
4	ice cubes	4

SUGGESTED TOPPINGS

Sliced banana

Sliced peaches

Sesame seeds

Ground flax seeds (flaxseed meal)

1. In blender, combine water, vanilla and protein powder. Secure lid and blend (from low to high if using a variable-speed blender) until smooth. Add banana, peaches, spinach and ice; blend until smooth.

2. Pour into bowls and top with any of the suggested toppings, as desired.

Variation

Replace the spinach with an equal amount of trimmed kale leaves.

Peach and Oat Bowl

This refreshing smoothie combines spinach, peaches and oats to create a treat for breakfast or lunch, or to rejuvenate after a tough workout.

MAKES 1 SERVING

Tip

Make sure this smoothie is blended well to incorporate the spinach, oats and chia seeds.

⅓ cup	water	75 mL
¼ cup	large-flake (old-fashioned) rolled oats	60 mL
2 tsp	chia seeds	10 mL
1	frozen banana, cut into pieces if necessary (see page 14)	1
1	peach, sliced	1
2 cups	trimmed spinach leaves	500 mL
	Ice cubes (optional)	

SUGGESTED TOPPINGS

Sliced banana

Sliced peach

Rolled oats

Hemp seeds

Chia seeds

1. In blender, combine water, oats, chia seeds, banana, peach and spinach. Secure lid and blend (from low to high if using a variable-speed blender) until smooth. If a thicker consistency is desired, add ice, one cube at a time, and blend until smooth.

2. Pour into a bowl and top with any of the suggested toppings, as desired.

Beauty Bowl

This pretty smoothie bowl is filled with ingredients that are great for your skin, including blueberries, cantaloupe, spinach, flax seeds and coconut water.

Tip

The best way to choose a cantaloupe is by smelling it. It should smell sweet.

¼ cup	coconut water	60 mL
½ tsp	ground flax seeds (flaxseed meal)	2 mL
½	frozen banana, cut into pieces if necessary (see page 14)	½
1½ cups	chopped cantaloupe	375 mL
½ cup	trimmed spinach leaves	125 mL
⅓ cup	blueberries	75 mL
	Ice cubes (optional)	

SUGGESTED TOPPINGS

Sliced banana

Sliced cantaloupe

Blueberries

Chopped pistachios

Ground flax seeds (flaxseed meal)

1. In blender, combine coconut water, flax seeds, banana, cantaloupe, spinach and blueberries. Secure lid and blend (from low to high if using a variable-speed blender) until smooth. If a thicker consistency is desired, add ice, one cube at a time, and blend until smooth.

2. Pour into bowls and top with any of the suggested toppings, as desired.

Basil Melon Bowl

This is one of my favorite green smoothie bowl recipes, filled with clean, fresh and flavorful ingredients.

Tip

Don't wash basil until right before you're about to use it, so it will not get wilted or turn brown.

¼ cup	water	60 mL
1 tbsp	liquid honey	15 mL
1	frozen banana, cut into pieces if necessary (see page 14)	1
2 cups	trimmed baby spinach leaves	500 mL
1 cup	chopped honeydew melon or cantaloupe	250 mL
¼ cup	chopped seeded cucumber	60 mL
¼ cup	fresh basil leaves	60 mL
	Ice cubes (optional)	

SUGGESTED TOPPINGS

Sliced banana

Chopped honeydew melon or cantaloupe

Sliced cucumber

Chopped fresh basil

1. In blender, combine water, honey, banana, spinach, melon, cucumber and basil. Secure lid and blend (from low to high if using a variable-speed blender) until smooth. If a thicker consistency is desired, add ice, one cube at a time, and blend until smooth.

2. Pour into a bowl or bowls and top with any of the suggested toppings, as desired.

Green Zinger

This pretty green smoothie is packed with ingredients that boost immunity.

Tips

Store unpeeled gingerroot in the refrigerator, tightly sealed in a plastic bag, for up to 2 weeks. Use it in stir-fries, marinades, sushi and smoothies.

If you prefer, you can use store-bought banana chips and granola to top your smoothie bowl.

¼ cup	coconut water	60 mL
1	frozen banana, cut into pieces if necessary (see page 14)	1
2	kiwifruit, peeled	2
2 cups	chopped honeydew melon	500 mL
1 tsp	grated gingerroot	5 mL
	Ice cubes (optional)	

SUGGESTED TOPPINGS

Sliced banana

Sliced kiwifruit

Banana Chips (page 208)

Cherry Almond Granola (page 215)

Chia seeds

1. In blender, combine coconut water, banana, kiwi, melon and ginger. Secure lid and blend (from low to high if using a variable-speed blender) until smooth. If a thicker consistency is desired, add ice, one cube at a time, and blend until smooth.

2. Pour into a bowl and top with any of the suggested toppings, as desired.

Melon Mango Refresher

Mint is a great palate cleanser and pairs well with just about any fruit, like the mango and melon in this smoothie bowl recipe.

Tip

If you have a large bunch of mint, store it in the refrigerator with the stems submerged in a glass of water. Place a plastic bag over the leaves, and it should keep up to 1 week.

½ cup	plain Greek yogurt	125 mL
¼ cup	coconut water	60 mL
1 cup	frozen chopped mango	250 mL
1 cup	trimmed kale leaves	250 mL
¾ cup	chopped honeydew melon	175 mL
1 tbsp	fresh mint	15 mL
4	ice cubes	4

SUGGESTED TOPPINGS

Chopped honeydew melon

Blueberries

Chia seeds

Chopped fresh mint

1. In blender, combine yogurt, coconut water, mango and kale. Secure lid and blend (from low to high if using a variable-speed blender) until smooth. Add melon, mint and ice; blend until smooth.

2. Pour into a bowl and top with any of the suggested toppings, as desired.

Variation

Substitute frozen sliced peaches for the mango.

Watermelon Kale Bowl

Watermelon is packed with vitamins, minerals, nutrients and — you guessed it — water. This smoothie combines it with another nutritional powerhouse, kale.

MAKES 1 TO 2 SERVINGS

Tips

Wash kale thoroughly and store it in the refrigerator for up to 4 days.

If you prefer, you can use store-bought granola to top your smoothie bowl.

3 tbsp	water	45 mL
1 tsp	liquid honey	5 mL
½	frozen banana, cut into pieces if necessary (see page 14)	½
1 cup	chopped watermelon (fresh or frozen) or Watermelon Cubes (page 18)	250 mL
1 cup	trimmed kale leaves	250 mL
	Ice cubes (optional)	

SUGGESTED TOPPINGS

Chopped watermelon

Classic Granola (page 210)

Hemp seeds

Chia seeds

1. In blender, combine water, honey, banana, watermelon and kale. Secure lid and blend (from low to high if using a variable-speed blender) until smooth. If a thicker consistency is desired, add ice, one cube at a time, and blend until smooth.

2. Pour into a bowl or bowls and top with any of the suggested toppings, as desired.

Lime Pineapple Bowl

My friend Caroline really liked this one, as did her daughter, Louise, who was only a toddler at the time!

Tip

Choose firm cucumbers with bright-colored skin and no blemishes.

¼ cup	water	60 mL
3 tbsp	freshly squeezed lime juice	45 mL
1 tbsp	liquid honey	15 mL
1	frozen banana, cut into pieces if necessary (see page 14)	1
1 cup	frozen chopped pineapple	250 mL
½ cup	chopped seedless cucumber	125 mL
	Ice cubes (optional)	

SUGGESTED TOPPINGS

Chopped seedless cucumber

Grated lime zest

Coconut Granola (page 216)

Chopped pecans

1. In blender, combine water, lime juice, honey, banana, pineapple and cucumber. Secure lid and blend (from low to high if using a variable-speed blender) until smooth. If a thicker consistency is desired, add ice, one cube at a time, and blend until smooth.

2. Pour into a bowl or bowls and top with any of the suggested toppings, as desired.

Variation

Add ¼ cup (60 mL) fresh cilantro leaves if you like the taste of cilantro.

Apple Kale Bowl

An apple a day keeps the doctor away, they say. Paired with kale, the chances are even greater.

Tip

If you prefer, you can use store-bought banana chips and granola to top your smoothie bowl.

1 cup	plain Greek yogurt	250 mL
¼ cup	unsweetened apple juice or apple cider	60 mL
½	scoop vanilla-flavored protein powder	½
1	frozen banana, cut into pieces if necessary (see page 14)	1
1	apple, chopped	1
2 cups	trimmed kale leaves	500 mL
4	ice cubes	4

SUGGESTED TOPPINGS

Banana Chips (page 208)

Classic Granola (page 210)

Ground flax seeds (flaxseed meal)

1. In blender, combine yogurt, apple juice and protein powder. Secure lid and blend (from low to high if using a variable-speed blender) until smooth. Add banana, apple, kale and ice; blend until smooth.

2. Pour into a bowl and top with any of the suggested toppings, as desired.

Green Coconut Bowl

Kale is high in vitamins K, A and C, iron, calcium and fiber. I made this recipe for some of my kids' friends, and they loved it. Their moms couldn't believe they were eating a green smoothie bowl with kale.

MAKES 1 SERVING

Tips

Use leftover coconut milk in soup recipes, Thai recipes, hot chocolate and breakfast cereal.

If you prefer, you can use store-bought granola to top your smoothie bowl.

¼ cup	unsweetened coconut milk beverage	60 mL
½	frozen banana, cut into pieces if necessary (see page 14)	½
⅓ cup	frozen chopped mango	75 mL
1 cup	trimmed kale leaves	250 mL
2 tbsp	unsweetened shredded or flaked coconut	30 mL
	Ice cubes (optional)	

SUGGESTED TOPPINGS

Sliced banana

Blueberries

Raspberries

Unsweetened shredded or flaked coconut

Coconut Granola (page 216)

Chia seeds

1. In blender, combine coconut milk, banana, mango, kale and coconut. Secure lid and blend (from low to high if using a variable-speed blender) until smooth. If a thicker consistency is desired, add ice, one cube at a time, and blend until smooth.

2. Pour into a bowl and top with any of the suggested toppings, as desired.

Green Dragon Fruit Bowl

This smoothie bowl has a beautiful color and every bite offers delectable sweetness.

**MAKES
1 SERVING**

Tips

Look for fresh or frozen dragon fruit at specialty grocery stores, Asian markets or online. If you purchase fresh dragon fruit, freeze it in an airtight container to use in this recipe. If you use purchased frozen dragon fruit, remove it from the freezer and let stand for a few minutes. Cut the package open and squeeze out the fruit.

If you prefer, you can use store-bought granola to top your smoothie bowl.

¼ cup	unsweetened apple juice	60 mL
1	scoop protein powder	1
1 cup	frozen chopped dragon fruit	250 mL
1	ripe banana	1
1 cup	trimmed spinach or kale leaves	250 mL
4	ice cubes	4

SUGGESTED TOPPINGS

Sliced banana

Cherry Almond Granola (page 215)

Hemp seeds

Chia seeds

1. In blender, combine apple juice and protein powder. Secure lid and blend (from low to high if using a variable-speed blender) until smooth. Add dragon fruit, banana, kale and ice; blend until smooth.

2. Pour into a bowl and top with any of the suggested toppings, as desired.

Kiwi Orange Bowl

Kiwi provides many health benefits and is high in vitamins and minerals. Here, it combines with orange juice and spinach to create a cold-fighting smoothie bowl.

MAKES 1 TO 2 SERVINGS

Tip

Trim the stems off spinach leaves before adding them to your blender.

⅓ cup	freshly squeezed orange juice	75 mL
2 tsp	liquid honey	10 mL
1	frozen banana, cut into pieces if necessary (see page 14)	1
1	kiwifruit, peeled	1
1 cup	trimmed spinach leaves	250 mL
	Ice cubes (optional)	

SUGGESTED TOPPINGS

Sliced orange

Sliced banana

Sliced kiwifruit

Unsweetened flaked coconut

Coconut Granola (page 216)

1. In blender, combine orange juice, honey, banana, kiwi and spinach. Secure lid and blend (from low to high if using a variable-speed blender) until smooth. If a thicker consistency is desired, add ice, one cube at a time, and blend until smooth.

2. Pour into a bowl or bowls and top with any of the suggested toppings, as desired.

Kiwi and Kale Bowl

Peach, kiwi and pineapple add great flavor combined with the kale in this recipe. This is my kids' favorite green smoothie. I made it for a children's cooking class, and everyone loved it!

ᴼᵒ

**MAKES
2 SERVINGS**

Tips

Purchase chopped pineapple at the grocery store if you are short on time.

If you prefer, you can use store-bought granola to top your smoothie bowl.

¾ cup	plain Greek yogurt	175 mL
¼ cup	unsweetened almond milk	60 mL
½	scoop protein powder (optional)	½
1 cup	frozen sliced peaches	250 mL
2	kiwifruit, peeled	2
1	ripe banana	1
2 cups	chopped pineapple	500 mL
1½ cups	trimmed kale leaves	375 mL
	Ice cubes (optional)	

SUGGESTED TOPPINGS

Sliced kiwifruit

Sliced banana

Chopped pineapple

Coconut Granola (page 216)

1. In blender, combine yogurt, almond milk and protein powder (if using). Secure lid and blend (from low to high if using a variable-speed blender) until smooth. Add peaches, kiwis, banana, pineapple and kale; blend until smooth. If a thicker consistency is desired, add ice, one cube at a time, and blend until smooth.

2. Pour into bowls and top with any of the suggested toppings, as desired.

Green Mango Bowl

Start your day off right with this fresh combination of mango, kiwi, spinach, Greek yogurt and pineapple.

MAKES 2 SERVINGS

Tip

One medium pineapple yields about 3 cups (750 mL) chopped.

⅔ cup	plain Greek yogurt	150 mL
¼ cup	water	60 mL
¼ cup	unsweetened almond milk	60 mL
½	scoop protein powder (optional)	½
1 tsp	liquid honey	5 mL
2 cups	frozen mango cubes	500 mL
1½ cups	trimmed baby spinach leaves	375 mL
2	kiwifruit, peeled	2
1	ripe banana	1
½ cup	chopped pineapple	125 mL
	Ice cubes (optional)	

SUGGESTED TOPPINGS

Sliced kiwifruit

Sliced banana

Chopped pineapple

Kale Chips (page 209), crushed

Sliced almonds

1. In blender, combine yogurt, water, almond milk and protein powder (if using). Secure lid and blend (from low to high if using a variable-speed blender) until smooth. Add honey, mango, spinach, kiwis, banana and pineapple; blend until smooth. If a thicker consistency is desired, add ice, one cube at a time, and blend until smooth.

2. Pour into bowls and top with any of the suggested toppings, as desired.

Mango Avocado Bowl

This smoothie bowl is a great choice for breakfast or an afternoon snack. Avocados add a smooth texture, as well as vitamins and minerals.

**MAKES
1 SERVING**

Tip

If you don't have coconut water on hand, substitute ⅓ cup (75 mL) water and add 1 tsp (5 mL) liquid honey.

⅓ cup	coconut water	75 mL
1	scoop protein powder	1
½ cup	frozen chopped mango	125 mL
1	kiwifruit, peeled	1
½	avocado	½
1½ cups	trimmed kale leaves	375 mL
4	ice cubes	4

SUGGESTED TOPPINGS

Sliced kiwifruit

Classic Granola (page 210)

Hemp seeds

Ground flax seeds (flaxseed meal)

1. In blender, combine coconut water and protein powder. Secure lid and blend (from low to high if using a variable-speed blender) until smooth. Add mango, kiwi, avocado, kale and ice; blend until smooth.

2. Pour into a bowl and top with any of the suggested toppings, as desired.

Papaya Green Bowl

Papaya is a rich source of vitamin A, which is important for eye and skin health. Here, it combines with orange juice, honey, spinach and banana to create freshness in a bowl.

Tips

You can find frozen chopped papaya in the frozen fruit section of most grocery stores.

If you use a frozen banana in place of the ripe banana, omit the ice.

If you prefer, you can use store-bought granola to top your smoothie bowl.

⅓ cup	freshly squeezed orange juice	75 mL
1 tsp	liquid honey	5 mL
1½ cups	frozen chopped papaya	375 mL
½	ripe banana	½
1 cup	trimmed spinach leaves	250 mL
	Ice cubes (optional)	

SUGGESTED TOPPINGS

Sliced banana

Maple Cinnamon Granola (page 211)

1. In blender, combine orange juice, honey, papaya, banana and spinach. Secure lid and blend (from low to high if using a variable-speed blender) until smooth. If a thicker consistency is desired, add ice, one cube at a time, and blend until smooth.

2. Pour into a bowl and top with any of the suggested toppings, as desired.

Variation

Substitute 1 cup (250 mL) trimmed kale leaves for the spinach.

Green Pineapple Bowl

I love using ingredients that help boost immunity, including spinach, ginger, pineapple and flax seeds.

**MAKES
1 SERVING**

Tip

When peeling ginger-root, carefully remove the skin without slicing into the flesh.

¼ cup	coconut water	60 mL
1 tsp	ground flax seeds (flaxseed meal)	5 mL
1	frozen banana, cut into pieces if necessary (see page 14)	1
½	seedless cucumber, sliced	½
2 cups	trimmed spinach leaves	500 mL
½ cup	chopped pineapple	125 mL
1 tbsp	grated gingerroot	15 mL
4	ice cubes	4

SUGGESTED TOPPINGS

Sliced banana

Sliced cucumber

Chopped pineapple

Ground flax seeds (flaxseed meal)

1. In blender, combine coconut water, flax seeds, banana, cucumber, spinach, pineapple, ginger and ice. Secure lid and blend (from low to high if using a variable-speed blender) until smooth.

2. Pour into a bowl and top with any of the suggested toppings, as desired.

Caribbean Detox

This recipe is a great choice after a vacation, a weekend of overeating or any time you feel bloated or like you need a detox.

MAKES 1 SERVING

Tip

If you use frozen pineapple, you may not need to use any ice.

¼ cup	coconut water	60 mL
½ tsp	ground flax seeds (flaxseed meal)	2 mL
½	frozen banana, cut into pieces if necessary (see page 14)	½
1 cup	trimmed kale leaves	250 mL
1 cup	chopped pineapple (fresh or frozen)	250 mL
1 tsp	grated gingerroot	5 mL
	Ice cubes (optional)	

SUGGESTED TOPPINGS

Sliced banana

Chopped pineapple

Coconut Granola (page 216)

Ground flax seeds (flaxseed meal)

1. In blender, combine coconut water, flax seeds, banana, kale, pineapple and ginger. Secure lid and blend (from low to high if using a variable-speed blender) until smooth. If a thicker consistency is desired, add ice, one cube at a time, and blend until smooth.

2. Pour into a bowl and top with any of the suggested toppings, as desired.

Variation

Add 1 scoop of vanilla-flavored protein powder for added protein and to promote fullness. Blend it with the coconut water before adding the remaining ingredients.

Green Star Fruit Bowl

Star fruit, also called carambola, is loaded with vitamin C. Look for it in the produce section of your grocery store or at specialty grocery stores.

Tip

To slice a star fruit, use a vegetable peeler to trim off the edges. Slice off the ends, cut the star fruit into slices and remove the seeds.

¼ cup	water	60 mL
1 tsp	freshly squeezed lime juice	5 mL
1 tsp	liquid honey	5 mL
1 cup	frozen chopped mango	250 mL
1 cup	trimmed spinach leaves	250 mL
2	large star fruit, trimmed and seeded (see tip, at left)	2
½	ripe banana	½
4	ice cubes	4

SUGGESTED TOPPINGS

Sliced star fruit

Sliced banana

Grated lime zest

Green pumpkin seeds (pepitas)

1. In blender, combine water, lime juice, honey, mango and spinach. Secure lid and blend (from low to high if using a variable-speed blender) until smooth. Add star fruit, banana and ice; blend until smooth.

2. Pour into a bowl or bowls and top with any of the suggested toppings, as desired.

Variation

Two Bartlett pears can be substituted for the star fruit if you can't find star fruit or have leftover pears on hand.

Avacolada

This tastes amazing! It's like a piña colada, but the avocado adds an even creamier, thicker texture.

Tip

Choose limes that have a bright green color and are heavy for their size. Remove them from the refrigerator 15 minutes before you want to use them, and roll them on the counter before slicing to get the most juice out.

¼ cup	coconut water	60 mL
1 tbsp	freshly squeezed lime juice	15 mL
1 cup	chopped pineapple (fresh or frozen)	250 mL
1	avocado	1
1 cup	trimmed baby spinach leaves	250 mL
1 tbsp	unsweetened shredded or flaked coconut	15 mL
	Ice cubes	

SUGGESTED TOPPINGS

Chopped pineapple

Chopped avocado

Unsweetened shredded or flaked coconut

Sesame seeds

1. In blender, combine coconut water, lime juice, pineapple, avocado, spinach and coconut. Secure lid and blend (from low to high if using a variable-speed blender) until smooth. Add ice, one cube at a time, blending until the desired consistency is achieved.

2. Pour into a bowl and top with any of the suggested toppings, as desired.

Avocado Chocolate Bowl

The combination of avocado and chocolate may sound odd at first, but wait until you taste this scrumptious smoothie — you'll think you're eating chocolate pudding!

**MAKES
1 SERVING**

Tips

Any type of milk — dairy or nondairy — can be substituted for the almond milk.

Make sure your avocado is ripe before making this recipe.

⅓ cup	unsweetened almond milk	75 mL
1 tbsp	liquid honey	15 mL
3 tbsp	natural unsweetened cocoa powder (not Dutch process)	45 mL
1	frozen banana, cut into pieces if necessary (see page 14)	1
1	ripe avocado	1
4	ice cubes	4

SUGGESTED TOPPINGS

Natural unsweetened cocoa powder

Sliced banana

Pecan Granola (page 213)

Chocolate chips

1. In blender, combine almond milk, honey, cocoa powder, banana, avocado and ice. Secure lid and blend (from low to high if using a variable-speed blender) until smooth.

2. Pour into a bowl and top with any of the suggested toppings, as desired.

Arugula Cucumber Bowl

Arugula and cucumbers are two of my favorite vegetables. Combine them in a smoothie bowl with green grapes and banana for a fresh, clean breakfast, snack or dessert.

○○○

MAKES 1 TO 2 SERVINGS

Tips

If you prefer a sweeter smoothie bowl, add 1 tsp (5 mL) liquid honey.

Hemp seeds can be purchased at specialty grocery stores or health food stores, or online.

You can use store-bought granola or any of the granola recipes in this book (pages 210–218) to top your smoothie bowl.

¼ cup	water	60 mL
½	frozen banana, cut into pieces if necessary (see page 14)	½
¾ cup	frozen green grapes	175 mL
1 cup	arugula	250 mL
¾ cup	chopped seedless cucumber	175 mL
1 tsp	hemp seeds	5 mL
	Ice cubes (optional)	

SUGGESTED TOPPINGS

Sliced banana

Sliced green grapes

Granola

Hemp seeds

1. In blender, combine water, banana, grapes, arugula, cucumber and hemp seeds. Secure lid and blend (from low to high if using a variable-speed blender) until smooth. If a thicker consistency is desired, add ice, one cube at a time, and blend until smooth.

2. Pour into a bowl or bowls and top with any of the suggested toppings, as desired.

Cucumber, Honey and Lavender Bowl

Cucumber and lavender pair delightfully with mint and yogurt in this irresistible recipe.

Tips

If you can't find coconut yogurt, use vanilla-flavored Greek yogurt.

Choose organic lavender whenever possible, and make sure you use only culinary-grade lavender in recipes.

If you can't find fresh lavender, substitute 1½ tsp (7 mL) dried lavender or 1 tbsp (15 mL) chopped fresh basil.

If you prefer, you can use store-bought granola to top your smoothie bowl.

1 cup	coconut-flavored yogurt	250 mL
1 cup	unsweetened almond milk	250 mL
1 tbsp	liquid honey	15 mL
1	seedless cucumber, sliced	1
1 tbsp	chopped fresh mint	15 mL
1 tbsp	chopped fresh lavender	15 mL
4	ice cubes	4

SUGGESTED TOPPINGS

Classic Granola (page 210)
Chopped almonds or pecans
Hemp seeds
Chopped fresh lavender
Chopped fresh mint

1. In blender, combine yogurt, almond milk, honey, cucumber, mint, lavender and ice. Secure lid and blend (from low to high if using a variable-speed blender) until smooth.

2. Pour into bowls and top with any of the suggested toppings, as desired.

Kid-Friendly Smoothie Bowls

Almond Butter and Jelly Bowl

My oldest son always says, "This is as filling as a meal."

Tips

If you prefer, you can use store-bought almond butter in place of homemade.

You can substitute unsweetened almond milk if you prefer to use less sugar.

½ cup	sweetened almond milk	125 mL
1	frozen banana, cut into pieces if necessary (see page 14)	1
½ cup	Homemade Almond Butter (page 226)	125 mL
¼ cup	strawberry jam	60 mL

SUGGESTED TOPPINGS

Sliced banana

Peanut Butter Granola (page 212)

Almonds

1. In blender, combine almond milk, banana, almond butter and jam. Secure lid and blend (from low to high if using a variable-speed blender) until smooth.

2. Pour into a bowl and top with any of the suggested toppings, as desired.

Variation

Substitute peanut butter for the almond butter, and grape jelly for the strawberry jam.

Peanut Butter Cup

If your kids like peanut butter and chocolate, they'll be huge fans of this recipe!

¼ cup	sweetened vanilla-flavored almond milk	60 mL
2 tbsp	unsweetened cocoa powder	30 mL
1	frozen banana, cut into pieces if necessary (see page 14)	1
½ cup	peanut butter	125 mL
4	ice cubes	4

SUGGESTED TOPPINGS

Unsweetened cocoa powder

Sliced banana

Best-Ever Chocolate Oat Cookies (page 223), crumbled

Mini chocolate chips

1. In blender, combine almond milk, cocoa powder, banana, peanut butter and ice. Secure lid and blend (from low to high if using a variable-speed blender) until smooth.

2. Pour into a bowl or bowls and top with any of the suggested toppings, as desired.

Variation

Add 1 scoop of chocolate-flavored protein powder for additional protein and thickness. Blend it with the almond milk before adding the remaining ingredients.

Peanut Butter Paradise

Smooth and creamy, this recipe is a source of protein, healthy fats, fiber and vitamins, sure to get your kids' day off to an energetic start.

½ cup	vanilla-flavored Greek yogurt	125 mL
¼ cup	unsweetened almond milk or milk	60 mL
2 tsp	liquid honey	10 mL
1	frozen banana, cut into pieces if necessary (see page 14)	1
¼ cup	peanut butter	60 mL
4	ice cubes	4

MAKES 1 SERVING

Tip

For added peanut buttery flavor, you can substitute ½ cup (125 mL) peanut butter–flavored Greek yogurt for the vanilla-flavored yogurt.

SUGGESTED TOPPINGS

Sliced banana

Chopped pecans

Chia seeds

1. In blender, combine yogurt, almond milk, honey, banana, peanut butter and ice. Secure lid and blend (from low to high if using a variable-speed blender) until smooth.

2. Pour into a bowl and top with any of the suggested toppings, as desired.

Mocha Smoothie Bowl

If your older kids like the taste of coffee and chocolate, they will love this one. My teens do!

Tips

Look for Greek frozen yogurt where ice cream and sorbet are sold at your local grocery store.

Chill the coffee before making this recipe so the smoothie bowl stays thick and cold.

1¾ cups	vanilla-flavored Greek frozen yogurt	425 mL
¼ cup	brewed coffee, chilled	60 mL
¼ cup	sweetened soy milk	60 mL
1 tbsp	unsweetened cocoa powder	15 mL
4	ice cubes	4

SUGGESTED TOPPINGS

Unsweetened cocoa powder

Cocoa nibs

Chopped pecans

Whipped cream

1. In blender, combine yogurt, coffee, soy milk, cocoa and ice. Secure lid and blend (from low to high if using a variable-speed blender) until smooth.

2. Pour into bowls and top with any of the suggested toppings, as desired.

Variation

Substitute coffee-flavored Greek frozen yogurt or ice cream for the vanilla.

Bee-Nut Smoothie Bowl

This is a favorite of my two youngest kids, Leigh and Zachary.

**MAKES
1 SERVING**

Tip

Add 2 tbsp (30 mL) ground flax seeds (flaxseed meal) before the banana for healthy omega-3 fats and extra fiber.

¼ cup	milk	60 mL
2 tsp	liquid honey	10 mL
1	frozen banana, cut into pieces if necessary (see page 14)	1
½ cup	peanut butter	125 mL
4	ice cubes	4

SUGGESTED TOPPINGS

Ground cinnamon

Sliced banana

Peanut Butter Granola (page 212)

1. In blender, combine milk, honey, banana, peanut butter and ice. Secure lid and blend (from low to high if using a variable-speed blender) until smooth.

2. Pour into a bowl and top with any of the suggested toppings, as desired.

Blueberry Chia Bowl

This recipe, filled with healthy ingredients, is the perfect way to start any kid's day off on the right foot.

MAKES 1 SERVING

Tip

You can substitute vanilla-flavored Greek yogurt for the kefir.

¼ cup	vanilla-flavored kefir	60 mL
2 tsp	liquid honey	10 mL
1	frozen banana, cut into pieces if necessary (see page 14)	1
1 tsp	chia seeds	5 mL
1 cup	blueberries (fresh or frozen)	250 mL
	Ice cubes (optional)	

SUGGESTED TOPPINGS

Sliced bananas

Blueberries

Raspberries

Cashew and Cranberry Granola (page 214)

Chia seeds

1. In blender, combine kefir, honey, banana, chia seeds and blueberries. Secure lid and blend (from low to high if using a variable-speed blender) until smooth. If a thicker consistency is desired, add ice, one cube at a time, and blend until smooth.

2. Pour into a bowl and top with any of the suggested toppings, as desired.

Blueberry Applesauce Bowl

Applesauce — a kid favorite — adds ultimate thickness and a delicate apple flavor to this simple three-ingredient recipe, possibly the easiest one in the book.

○○

MAKES 2 SERVINGS

Tip

You can use 1½ cups (375 mL) of any favorite frozen fruit in place of the blueberries.

¾ cup	unsweetened applesauce	175 mL
1	frozen banana, cut into pieces if necessary (see page 14)	1
1½ cups	frozen blueberries	375 mL
	Ice cubes (optional)	

SUGGESTED TOPPINGS

Sliced banana

Blueberries

Raspberries

Unsweetened shredded coconut

Classic Granola (page 210)

Hemp seeds

Ground flax seeds (flaxseed meal)

1. In blender, combine applesauce, banana and blueberries. Secure lid and blend (from low to high if using a variable-speed blender) until smooth. If a thicker consistency is desired, add ice, one cube at a time, and blend until smooth.

2. Pour into bowls and top with any of the suggested toppings, as desired.

Love Potion

This smoothie bowl with truly vibrant color is fun to make for any loved one.

Tip

Use 100% pure pomegranate juice for the best health benefits and powerful pomegranate flavor.

¾ cup	plain Greek yogurt	175 mL
¼ cup	unsweetened pomegranate juice	60 mL
2 tbsp	agave syrup or liquid honey	30 mL
1 cup	frozen strawberries	250 mL
1 cup	raspberries (fresh or frozen)	250 mL
	Ice cubes (optional)	

SUGGESTED TOPPINGS

Sliced strawberries

Raspberries

Pomegranate seeds

Ground almonds

1. In blender, combine yogurt, pomegranate juice, agave syrup, strawberries and raspberries. Secure lid and blend (from low to high if using a variable-speed blender) until smooth. If a thicker consistency is desired, add ice, one cube at a time, and blend until smooth.

2. Pour into bowls and top with any of the suggested toppings, as desired.

Strawberry Peach Bowl

This recipe is really refreshing and a pretty color!

Tips

If you're following a gluten-free diet, use certified gluten-free oats.

If you don't have a fresh peach on hand, you can use frozen sliced peaches and omit the ice.

¼ cup	milk	60 mL
1 tbsp	large-flake (old-fashioned) rolled oats	15 mL
1 tsp	ground flax seeds (flaxseed meal)	5 mL
½	frozen banana, cut into pieces if necessary (see page 14)	½
1	peach, sliced	1
¾ cup	strawberries	175 mL
4	ice cubes	4

SUGGESTED TOPPINGS

Sliced banana

Sliced peach

Sliced strawberries

Hemp seeds

Ground flax seeds (flaxseed meal)

1. In blender, combine milk, oats, flax seeds, banana, peach, strawberries and ice. Secure lid and blend (from low to high if using a variable-speed blender) until smooth.

2. Pour into a bowl and top with any of the suggested toppings, as desired.

Berry Crunch

If your kids like crunch, this recipe is for them!

MAKES 2 SERVINGS

Tips

Toasting nuts brings out great flavor and adds crunch. Toast them in a dry skillet over medium heat, stirring frequently, until golden brown, or toast them in a preheated 350°F (180°C) oven, stirring occasionally, for 10 to 15 minutes or until golden brown. Let cool completely before adding them to the blender.

Soak the almonds before toasting if your kids like a less crunchy flavor for their smoothie bowls. Place them in a bowl, cover with warm water and let soak for 20 to 30 minutes; drain well and pat dry before toasting.

¼ cup	milk or unsweetened almond milk	60 mL
1	frozen banana, cut into pieces if necessary (see page 14)	1
¼ cup	toasted almonds (see tips, at left)	60 mL
¼ cup	toasted pecan halves	60 mL
¾ cup	strawberries (fresh or frozen)	175 mL
¾ cup	blueberries (fresh or frozen)	175 mL
	Ice cubes (optional)	

SUGGESTED TOPPINGS

Sliced strawberries

Sliced banana

Cherry Almond Granola (page 215)

Chopped toasted almonds

Chopped toasted pecans

1. In blender, combine milk and banana. Secure lid and blend (from low to high if using a variable-speed blender) until smooth. Add almonds, pecans, strawberries and blueberries; blend until smooth. If a thicker consistency is desired, add ice, one cube at a time, and blend until smooth.

2. Pour into bowls and top with any of the suggested toppings, as desired.

Variation

Add 1 scoop of protein powder for additional protein and thickness. Blend it with the milk before adding the remaining ingredients.

Berry Bliss

Kids who like berries will love this satisfying, pretty recipe.

	MAKES 1 SERVING	

Tip

You can use store-bought granola or any of the granola recipes in this book (pages 210–218) for this recipe.

¾ cup	vanilla-flavored Greek yogurt	175 mL
¼ cup	unsweetened almond milk	60 mL
1 tbsp	liquid honey	15 mL
½	frozen banana, cut into pieces if necessary (see page 14)	½
2 tbsp	granola	30 mL
1 cup	mixed berries (fresh or frozen)	250 mL
	Ice cubes (optional)	

SUGGESTED TOPPINGS

Sliced banana

Fresh berries

Granola

1. In blender, combine yogurt, almond milk, honey, banana, granola and berries. Secure lid and blend (from low to high if using a variable-speed blender) until smooth. If a thicker consistency is desired, add ice, one cube at a time, and blend until smooth.

2. Pour into a bowl and top with any of the suggested toppings, as desired.

Coco-Berry Bowl

Coconut milk and berries create a colorful and satisfying breakfast, ideal for a healthy start to your kids' day.

**MAKES
1 SERVING**

Tips

You can substitute ⅓ cup (75 mL) coconut water or milk for the coconut milk beverage. If using milk, add 2 tbsp (30 mL) unsweetened shredded coconut with the frozen fruit.

Toast coconut in a preheated 350°F (180°C) oven for 6 to 8 minutes (or under the broiler for 2 minutes), until lightly browned.

⅓ cup	unsweetened coconut milk beverage	75 mL
1 tsp	liquid honey	5 mL
1	frozen banana, cut into pieces if necessary (see page 14)	1
1 cup	frozen blueberries	250 mL
1 cup	frozen strawberries	250 mL

SUGGESTED TOPPINGS

Sliced banana

Blueberries

Sliced strawberries

Toasted unsweetened shredded coconut (see tip, at left)

Pecan Granola (page 213)

Hemp seeds

1. In blender, combine coconut milk, honey, banana, blueberries and strawberries. Secure lid and blend (from low to high if using a variable-speed blender) until smooth.

2. Pour into a bowl and top with any of the suggested toppings, as desired.

Grape Ape

Grapes are a rich source of vitamins A, C and B_6 and make a wonderfully healthy and flavorful fruit addition to smoothie bowls. Plus, kids love them!

Tips

Store grapes unwashed in the refrigerator. They will spoil faster if you wash them right after purchasing them.

For a rich purple smoothie bowl, use red grapes. Green grapes will result in a greener color.

½ cup	vanilla-flavored Greek yogurt	125 mL
¼ cup	unsweetened apple juice	60 mL
1	frozen banana, cut into pieces if necessary (see page 14)	1
1 cup	seedless red or green grapes (or a mixture)	250 mL
4	ice cubes	4

SUGGESTED TOPPINGS

Sliced grapes

Banana Chips (page 208)

Kitchen Sink Granola (page 218)

1. In blender, combine yogurt, apple juice, banana, grapes and ice. Secure lid and blend (from low to high if using a variable-speed blender) until smooth.

2. Pour into a bowl and top with any of the suggested toppings, as desired.

Variation

Add 1 tbsp (15 mL) protein powder for additional protein and thickness. Blend it with the liquids before adding the remaining ingredients.

Chocolate Cherry Bowl

Chocolate and cherries are a delectable combination that will have your kids wanting seconds.

Tip

If you use fresh cherries, you'll definitely need to add some ice, one cube at a time.

¾ cup	vanilla-flavored Greek yogurt	175 mL
1 tbsp	unsweetened cocoa powder	15 mL
½	frozen banana, cut into pieces if necessary (see page 14)	½
1 cup	frozen cherries	250 mL
	Ice cubes (optional)	

SUGGESTED TOPPINGS

Raw cacao powder

Sliced banana

Pitted cherries

Classic Granola (page 210)

Chopped walnuts

1. In blender, combine yogurt, cocoa, banana and cherries. Secure lid and blend (from low to high if using a variable-speed blender) until smooth. If a thicker consistency is desired, add ice, one cube at a time, and blend until smooth.

2. Pour into a bowl and top with any of the suggested toppings, as desired.

Variations

If you can't find fresh or frozen cherries, you can substitute strawberries.

For an even more chocolatey flavor, add ¼ cup (60 mL) chocolate milk.

Apple Cider Bowl

Serve this fall favorite at any autumnal gathering, brunch or Halloween party.

MAKES 2 SERVINGS

Tips

Purchase pure apple cider, found chilled in the produce section at most grocery stores.

If you can't find Honeycrisp apples, try Golden Delicious, Braeburn, Fuji or even Red Delicious.

½ cup	unsweetened applesauce	125 mL
¼ cup	unsweetened apple cider	60 mL
½ tsp	ground cinnamon	2 mL
1	frozen banana, cut into pieces if necessary (see page 14)	1
1½ cups	chopped Honeycrisp or other sweet apples	375 mL
	Ice cubes (optional)	

SUGGESTED TOPPINGS

Ground cinnamon

Sliced apple

Apple Chips (page 208)

Maple Cinnamon Granola (page 211)

Chopped pecans

Chopped walnuts

Hemp seeds

Chia seeds

1. In blender, combine applesauce, apple cider, cinnamon, banana and apples. Secure lid and blend (from low to high if using a variable-speed blender) until smooth. If a thicker consistency is desired, add ice, one cube at a time, and blend until smooth.

2. Pour into bowls and top with any of the suggested toppings, as desired.

Peachy Morning Smoothie Bowl

This peachy recipe will start your kids' day off right or end it on a sweet note.

Tip

When selecting peaches, choose those that are fragrant and give slightly to palm pressure. Avoid peaches that are hard.

½ cup	vanilla-flavored Greek yogurt	125 mL
3 tbsp	milk or unsweetened almond milk	45 mL
1 tsp	liquid honey	5 mL
1	frozen banana, cut into pieces if necessary (see page 14)	1
1 cup	sliced peaches (fresh or frozen)	250 mL
	Ice cubes (optional)	

SUGGESTED TOPPINGS

Sliced banana

Sliced peach

Classic Granola (page 210)

Ground flax seeds (flaxseed meal)

1. In blender, combine yogurt, milk, honey, banana and peaches. Secure lid and blend (from low to high if using a variable-speed blender) until smooth. If a thicker consistency is desired, add ice, one cube at a time, and blend until smooth.

2. Pour into a bowl and top with any of the suggested toppings, as desired.

Variation

For a dairy-free version, substitute coconut yogurt for the vanilla yogurt, and unsweetened coconut milk beverage for the milk.

Peach Paradise

My kids love this smoothie bowl as an after-dinner dessert or for breakfast.

MAKES 2 SERVINGS

Tip

If fresh peaches are not in season, use 1½ cups (375 mL) frozen sliced peaches and omit the ice.

¼ cup	milk	60 mL
1 tsp	liquid honey	5 mL
½	frozen banana, cut into pieces if necessary (see page 14)	½
2	peaches, sliced (see tip, at left)	2
½ cup	chopped pineapple	125 mL
4	ice cubes	4

SUGGESTED TOPPINGS

Sliced banana

Sliced peach

Chopped pineapple

Chopped pecans

1. In blender, combine milk, honey, banana, peaches, pineapple and ice. Secure lid and blend (from low to high if using a variable-speed blender) until smooth.

2. Pour into bowls and top with any of the suggested toppings, as desired.

Peachy King

This smoothie bowl, with a pretty peach color, is very refreshing. It's the perfect snack for kids after athletic activities.

MAKES 1 SERVING

Tip

For added nutrition and fiber, add 1 tsp (5 mL) ground flax seeds (flaxseed meal) after the honey.

¼ cup	unsweetened vanilla-flavored almond milk	60 mL
1 tbsp	liquid honey	15 mL
½	frozen banana, cut into pieces if necessary (see page 14)	½
½ cup	frozen sliced strawberries	125 mL
½ cup	sliced peaches (fresh or frozen)	125 mL
	Ice cubes (optional)	

SUGGESTED TOPPINGS

Sliced banana

Strawberries

Sliced peach

Pecan Granola (page 213)

1. In blender, combine almond milk, honey, banana, strawberries and peaches. Secure lid and blend (from low to high if using a variable-speed blender) until smooth. If a thicker consistency is desired, add ice, one cube at a time, and blend until smooth.

2. Pour into a bowl and top with any of the suggested toppings, as desired.

Variation

Add 1 tbsp (15 mL) goji berries after the banana to enhance this smoothie bowl's color and flavor.

Peach and Pineapple Bowl

If your kids like peaches and pineapple, they'll savor this smoothie bowl.

Tips

If you can't find white cranberry and peach juice drink, substitute ½ cup (125 mL) peach nectar.

You can purchase dried white peaches at specialty grocery stores, health food stores or online.

½ cup	white cranberry and peach juice drink	125 mL
1	frozen banana, cut into pieces if necessary (see page 14)	1
1½ cups	frozen sliced peaches	375 mL
½ cup	frozen chopped pineapple	125 mL

SUGGESTED TOPPINGS

Sliced banana

Chopped dried white peaches

Toasted unsweetened shredded coconut (see tip, page 109)

Easy Muesli (page 219)

Chopped pecans

Honey- and sesame–covered almonds

1. In blender, combine cranberry juice, banana, peaches and pineapple. Secure lid and blend (from low to high if using a variable-speed blender) until smooth.

2. Pour into a bowl and top with any of the suggested toppings, as desired.

Variation

Substitute ½ cup (125 mL) white peach sorbet for the cranberry juice.

Orange, Banana and Coconut Bowl

My kids love this one, and I love serving it when they have friends over. It is so tasty that you may need to double the recipe, as they always request more than one serving each.

	MAKES 1 SERVING	

Tip

Before juicing or slicing an orange, grate all the zest. Store leftover zest in an airtight plastic bag in the freezer, so you have it on hand whenever a recipe calls for it.

2 tbsp	freshly squeezed orange juice	30 mL
2 tbsp	milk	30 mL
3 tbsp	large-flake (old-fashioned) rolled oats	45 mL
1	frozen banana, cut into pieces if necessary (see page 14)	1
1 cup	sliced oranges	250 mL
2 tbsp	unsweetened shredded coconut	30 mL
4	ice cubes	4

SUGGESTED TOPPINGS

Sliced banana
Unsweetened shredded coconut
Grated orange zest
Classic Granola (page 210)

1. In blender, combine orange juice, milk, oats, banana, oranges, coconut and ice. Secure lid and blend (from low to high if using a variable-speed blender) until smooth.

2. Pour into a bowl and top with any of the suggested toppings, as desired.

Variation

Add 1 tbsp (15 mL) protein powder for additional protein and thickness. Blend it with the liquids before adding the remaining ingredients.

Banana Oat Bowl

My daughter, Leigh, came up with this recipe. It's one of her go-to breakfasts.

	MAKES 1 SERVING	

Tip

Add 1 tsp (5 mL) chia seeds with the oats. Chia seeds are a good source of alpha-linolenic acid, an omega-3 fatty acid that helps support cardiovascular health, and fiber, which helps with digestive health.

¼ cup	milk	60 mL
1 tsp	liquid honey	5 mL
1	scoop protein powder	1
¼ cup	large-flake (old-fashioned) rolled oats	60 mL
1	frozen banana, cut into pieces if necessary (see page 14)	1
4	ice cubes	4

SUGGESTED TOPPINGS

Ground cinnamon

Sliced banana

Rolled oats

Maple Cinnamon Granola (page 211)

Chopped pecans

1. In blender, combine milk, honey and protein powder. Secure lid and blend (from low to high if using a variable-speed blender) until smooth. Add oats, banana and ice; blend until smooth.

2. Pour into a bowl and top with any of the suggested toppings, as desired.

Chocolate Banana Bowl

This four-ingredient smoothie is perfect for breakfast or after school.

**MAKES
1 SERVING**

Tips

Substitute chocolate milk or any other chocolate-flavored nondairy milk for the soy milk.

If you prefer not to use nuts or avoid them because of allergies, substitute 1 tbsp (15 mL) hemp seeds in place of the pecans.

¼ cup	sweetened chocolate-flavored soy milk	60 mL
1 tbsp	unsweetened cocoa powder	15 mL
1	frozen banana, cut into pieces if necessary (see page 14)	1
1 tbsp	chopped pecans	15 mL
4	ice cubes	4

SUGGESTED TOPPINGS

Unsweetened cocoa powder

Sliced banana

Chopped pecans

Mini chocolate chips

1. In blender, combine soy milk, cocoa, banana, pecans and ice. Secure lid and blend (from low to high if using a variable-speed blender) until smooth.

2. Pour into a bowl and top with any of the suggested toppings, as desired.

Chocolate Hazelnut Banana Bowl

Hazelnut flavor is abundant in this rich and creamy smoothie bowl.

½ cup	vanilla-flavored Greek yogurt	125 mL
2 tbsp	unsweetened almond milk	30 mL
½	frozen banana, cut into pieces if necessary (see page 14)	½
¼ cup	chocolate-hazelnut spread	60 mL
4	ice cubes	4

MAKES 1 SERVING

Tip

You can use store-bought granola or any of the granola recipes in this book (pages 210–218) to top your smoothie bowl.

SUGGESTED TOPPINGS

Unsweetened cocoa powder

Sliced banana

Granola

Chopped cashews

Chopped hazelnuts

1. In blender, combine yogurt, almond milk, banana, chocolate-hazelnut spread and ice. Secure lid and blend (from low to high if using a variable-speed blender) until smooth.

2. Pour into a bowl and top with any of the suggested toppings, as desired.

Variations

If your kids like a sweeter taste, add 2 tsp (10 mL) liquid honey after the almond milk.

Add 2 tbsp (30 mL) Cinnamon Cashew Nut Butter (page 228) before the ice.

Banana Cashew Bowl

My daughter, Leigh, loves this one. It's great for an afternoon snack!

Tips

Peel and freeze overripe bananas in sealable plastic bags.

If you prefer, you can use store-bought banana chips and granola to top your smoothie bowl.

You can substitute Homemade Almond Butter (page 226) or store-bought cashew butter, almond butter or peanut butter for the homemade cashew butter.

¼ cup	unsweetened almond milk or milk	60 mL
1 tsp	liquid honey	5 mL
1	frozen banana, cut into pieces if necessary (see page 14)	1
½ cup	Cinnamon Cashew Nut Butter (page 228)	125 mL
4	ice cubes	4

SUGGESTED TOPPINGS

Sliced banana

Banana Chips (page 208)

Cashew and Cranberry Granola (page 214)

Chopped cashews

1. In blender, combine milk, honey, banana, cashew butter and ice. Secure lid and blend (from low to high if using a variable-speed blender) until smooth.

2. Pour into a bowl and top with any of the suggested toppings, as desired.

Coconut Banana Bowl

This decadent smoothie bowl is similar to a sorbet and makes a very refreshing dessert or breakfast.

MAKES 2 SERVINGS

Tip

Unsweetened shredded coconut is the preferred choice for this recipe, since there is already honey in it, but you can use sweetened coconut to indulge a sweet tooth.

¼ cup	coconut water	60 mL
1 tsp	liquid honey	5 mL
1	frozen banana, cut into pieces if necessary (see page 14)	1
¾ cup	chopped pineapple (fresh or frozen)	175 mL
2 tbsp	unsweetened shredded coconut (see tip, at left)	30 mL
4	ice cubes	4

SUGGESTED TOPPINGS

Sliced banana

Coconut Granola (page 216)

Ground flax seeds (flaxseed meal)

1. In blender, combine coconut water, honey, banana, pineapple, coconut and ice. Secure lid and blend (from low to high if using a variable-speed blender) until smooth.

2. Pour into bowls and top with any of the suggested toppings, as desired.

Kiwi Strawberry Bowl

The kid-friendly combination of kiwi and strawberry makes a refreshing treat for a summertime breakfast.

MAKES 2 SERVINGS

Tip

To peel kiwifruit, use a paring knife, vegetable peeler or serrated knife.

½ cup	plain Greek yogurt	125 mL
2 tbsp	water	30 mL
2 tsp	liquid honey	2 mL
1	frozen banana, cut into pieces if necessary (see page 14)	1
2	kiwifruit, peeled	2
¾ cup	strawberries	175 mL
4	ice cubes	4

SUGGESTED TOPPINGS

Sliced kiwifruit

Sliced strawberries

Sliced banana

Chopped toasted almonds

1. In blender, combine yogurt, water, honey, banana, kiwis, strawberries and ice. Secure lid and blend (from low to high if using a variable-speed blender) until smooth.

2. Pour into bowls and top with any of the suggested toppings, as desired.

Variation

For a dairy-free version, substitute ½ cup (125 mL) coconut water and omit the yogurt and water.

Mango Berry Bowl

This smoothie bowl has fabulous color and flavor, perfect for a kid-approved breakfast or afternoon snack.

Tip

You can substitute milk or unsweetened almond milk for the coconut milk beverage.

⅓ cup	sweetened coconut milk beverage	75 mL
1 cup	frozen chopped mango	250 mL
1 cup	blueberries or raspberries (fresh or frozen)	250 mL
½	ripe banana	½
	Ice cubes (optional)	

SUGGESTED TOPPINGS

Blueberries

Raspberries

Sliced banana

Goji berries

Unsweetened shredded coconut

Ground flax seeds (flaxseed meal)

1. In blender, combine coconut milk, mango, blueberries and banana. Secure lid and blend (from low to high if using a variable-speed blender) until smooth. If a thicker consistency is desired, add ice, one cube at a time, and blend until smooth.

2. Pour into a bowl and top with any of the suggested toppings, as desired.

Pineapple Sunrise

This fruity and tropical recipe is a bowl of morning sunshine.

Tip

Hemp seeds are rich in protein, omega-3 fatty acids, fiber and magnesium.

2 tbsp	freshly squeezed orange juice	30 mL
2 tbsp	water	30 mL
2 tsp	protein powder	10 mL
1	frozen banana, cut into pieces if necessary (see page 14)	1
1 cup	chopped pineapple (fresh or frozen)	250 mL
1 tsp	hemp seeds	5 mL
	Ice cubes (optional)	

SUGGESTED TOPPINGS

Sliced banana

Chopped pineapple

Coconut Granola (page 216)

Hemp seeds

1. In blender, combine orange juice, water and protein powder. Secure lid and blend (from low to high if using a variable-speed blender) until smooth. Add banana, pineapple and hemp seeds; blend until smooth. If a thicker consistency is desired, add ice, one cube at a time, and blend until smooth.

2. Pour into a bowl or bowls and top with any of the suggested toppings, as desired.

Variations

Substitute pineapple juice for the orange juice.

Replace the protein powder with 1 tbsp (15 mL) large-flake (old-fashioned) rolled oats.

Hawaiian Smoothie Bowl

Your kids will love this tropical smoothie bowl made with papaya, coconut water, banana and pineapple — it's a taste of Hawaii!

½ cup	coconut water	125 mL
1	frozen banana, cut into pieces if necessary (see page 14)	1
1 cup	frozen chopped papaya	250 mL
1 cup	frozen chopped pineapple	250 mL

(see page 14)

**MAKES
2 SERVINGS**

Tip

Look for sesame- and honey-covered almonds or cashews where trail mix and granola are sold in specialty grocery stores or online. If you can't find them, use regular almonds or cashews.

SUGGESTED TOPPINGS

Sliced banana

Dried pineapple pieces

Unsweetened shredded coconut

Chopped macadamia nuts

Sesame- and honey-covered almonds or cashews

1. In blender, combine coconut water, banana, papaya and pineapple. Secure lid and blend (from low to high if using a variable-speed blender) until smooth.

2. Pour into bowls and top with any of the suggested toppings, as desired.

Variation

For even more tropical flavor, substitute ½ cup (125 mL) guava nectar for the coconut water.

Kale Pineapple Bowl

My three kids all love this one — it's a true family favorite.

Tips

You can freeze kale without blanching it first, but use it within 4 to 6 weeks. Be sure to write the date on the outside of your freezer bag. If you use frozen kale in this recipe, omit the ice.

If you prefer, you can use store-bought granola to top your smoothie bowl.

¼ cup	unsweetened pineapple juice	60 mL
1	frozen banana, cut into pieces if necessary (see page 14)	1
1 cup	frozen chopped pineapple	250 mL
1 cup	chopped trimmed kale leaves	250 mL
	Ice cubes (optional)	

SUGGESTED TOPPINGS

Sliced banana

Chopped pineapple

Unsweetened shredded coconut

Coconut Granola (page 216)

1. In blender, combine pineapple juice, banana, pineapple and kale. Secure lid and blend (from low to high if using a variable-speed blender) until smooth. If a thicker consistency is desired, add ice, one cube at a time, and blend until smooth.

2. Pour into bowls and top with any of the suggested toppings, as desired.

Variation

Add 1 scoop of protein powder for additional protein and thickness. Blend it with the pineapple juice before adding the remaining ingredients.

Layered Smoothie Bowl

Layered smoothies take a little extra time, but they are so worth it.

¾ cup	coconut water, divided	175 mL
1 cup	frozen chopped mango	250 mL
½ cup	sliced peaches (fresh or frozen)	125 mL
1 tsp	freshly squeezed lime juice	5 mL
1	frozen banana, cut into pieces if necessary (see page 14)	1
1 cup	sliced strawberries	250 mL

MAKES 1 TO 2 SERVINGS

Tip

If you decide not to create a layered smoothie bowl, just blend everything at once.

SUGGESTED TOPPINGS

Sliced strawberries

Sliced banana

Unsweetened shredded coconut

Chopped pecans

1. In blender, combine ½ cup (125 mL) coconut water, mango and peaches. Secure lid and blend (from low to high if using a variable-speed blender) until smooth. Pour into a bowl or bowls.

2. Clean blender, then combine the remaining coconut water, lime juice, banana and strawberries. Secure lid and blend (from low to high if using a variable-speed blender) until smooth.

3. Carefully pour strawberry layer on top of mango layer. Top with any of the suggested toppings, as desired.

Anytime Smoothie Bowls

Almond Butter and Strawberry Bowl

This smoothie bowl is fabulous after a morning or afternoon workout!

MAKES 1 SERVING

Tips

If you prefer, you can use store-bought almond butter in place of homemade.

A 10-oz (300 g) package of blueberries equals 1½ cups (375 mL).

¼ cup	unsweetened almond milk	60 mL
1	frozen banana, cut into pieces if necessary (see page 14)	1
¾ cup	strawberries (fresh or frozen)	175 mL
½ cup	blueberries (fresh or frozen)	125 mL
1 tbsp	Homemade Almond Butter (page 226)	15 mL
	Ice cubes (optional)	

SUGGESTED TOPPINGS

Strawberries

Blueberries

Almonds

Chia seeds

Ground flax seeds (flaxseed meal)

1. In blender, combine almond milk, banana, strawberries, blueberries and almond butter. Secure lid and blend (from low to high if using a variable-speed blender) until smooth. If a thicker consistency is desired, add ice, one cube at a time, and blend until smooth.

2. Pour into a bowl and top with any of the suggested toppings, as desired.

Variation

Add 1 tbsp (15 mL) protein powder for additional thickness and protein. Blend it with the almond milk before adding the remaining ingredients.

Coconut Macadamia Nut Bowl

Macadamia nuts are often overlooked in the nut category, but they are a rich source of energy. They pair well with the banana, coconut and honey in this recipe.

Tips

Toast the macadamia nuts in a dry skillet over medium heat, stirring frequently, until golden brown, or toast them in a preheated 350°F (180°C) oven, stirring occasionally, for 10 to 15 minutes or until golden brown. Let cool completely before adding them to the blender.

Soak macadamia nuts before toasting them if you like a less crunchy texture for your smoothie bowls. Place them in a bowl, cover with warm water and let soak for 20 to 30 minutes; drain well and pat dry before toasting.

¼ cup	coconut milk	60 mL
1 tsp	liquid honey	5 mL
1 tbsp	vanilla-flavored protein powder	15 mL
1	frozen banana, cut into pieces if necessary (see page 14)	1
½ cup	toasted macadamia nuts (see tips, at left)	125 mL
2 tbsp	unsweetened flaked coconut	30 mL
4	ice cubes	4

SUGGESTED TOPPINGS

Sliced banana

Unsweetened flaked coconut

Coconut Granola (page 216)

Macadamia nuts

1. In blender, combine milk, honey and protein powder. Secure lid and blend (from low to high if using a variable-speed blender) until smooth. Add banana, macadamia nuts, coconut and ice; blend until smooth.

2. Pour into a bowl and top with any of the suggested toppings, as desired.

Pistachio Vanilla Bowl

Did you know that pistachios are high in potassium and fiber? What's more, they make a fabulous smoothie bowl ingredient.

○○

¾ cup	unsweetened vanilla-flavored almond milk	175 mL
2 tsp	liquid honey	10 mL
1	scoop vanilla-flavored protein powder	1
1	frozen banana, cut into pieces if necessary (see page 14)	1
⅓ cup	pistachios, soaked and drained (see tips, at left)	75 mL
	Ice cubes (optional)	

MAKES 1 SERVING

Tips

I prefer to use raw pistachios in my smoothie bowls. If you can't find them, use unsalted roasted pistachios.

To soak pistachios, place them in a bowl, cover with warm water and let soak for 20 to 30 minutes; drain well before adding them to the blender.

If you don't have time to soak the pistachios, add them unsoaked and blend them with the milk, honey and protein powder.

SUGGESTED TOPPINGS

Matcha powder

Ground cinnamon

Sliced banana

Pistachios

1. In blender, combine milk, honey and protein powder. Secure lid and blend (from low to high if using a variable-speed blender) until smooth. Add banana and pistachios; blend until smooth. If a thicker consistency is desired, add ice, one cube at a time, and blend until smooth.

2. Pour into a bowl and top with any of the suggested toppings, as desired.

Classic Açaí Smoothie Bowl

My kids and I have been drinking açaí smoothies for years, but now we love making our own açaí smoothie bowls at home.

MAKES 1 TO 2 SERVINGS

Tips

Purchase frozen açaí purée in packages at gourmet grocery stores, online or at health food stores. Be sure to buy pure, unsweetened purée.

If you prefer, you can use store-bought granola to top your smoothie bowl.

¼ cup	water	60 mL
1½	packages (each 3½ oz/100 g) frozen açaí purée	1½
½	frozen banana, cut into pieces if necessary (see page 14)	½
1 cup	sliced strawberries	250 mL
½ cup	blueberries	125 mL
	Ice cubes (optional)	

SUGGESTED TOPPINGS

Sliced banana

Strawberries

Blueberries

Goji berries

Dried mulberries

Classic Granola (page 210)

1. In blender, combine water, açaí and banana. Secure lid and blend (from low to high if using a variable-speed blender) until smooth. Add strawberries and blueberries; blend until smooth. If a thicker consistency is desired, add ice, one cube at a time, and blend until smooth.

2. Pour into a bowl or bowls and top with any of the suggested toppings, as desired.

Açaí Avocado Bowl

Adding avocado to smoothie bowls gives them a creamier and thicker texture. Some people avoid avocados because of their high fat content, but it is the heart-friendly monounsaturated type of fat. My kids would never know there's an avocado in this recipe.

MAKES 1 TO 2 SERVINGS

Tip

It is frustrating when you can only find underripe avocados at your local grocery store. Speed up the ripening process by placing several avocados in a paper bag with an apple. Pierce the bag with a fork in several places (without piercing the avocados or apple) and store at room temperature for 1 to 3 days, checking each day for ripeness.

¼ cup	water	60 mL
1½	packages (each 3½ oz/100 g) frozen açaí purée	1½
½	frozen banana, cut into pieces if necessary (see page 14)	½
½	avocado	½
¾ cup	strawberries	175 mL
	Ice cubes (optional)	

SUGGESTED TOPPINGS

Sliced banana

Sliced strawberries

Classic Granola (page 210)

Chia seeds

Hemp seeds

1. In blender, combine water, acai and banana. Secure lid and blend (from low to high if using a variable-speed blender) until smooth. Add avocado and strawberries; blend until smooth. If a thicker consistency is desired, add ice, one cube at a time, and blend until smooth.

2. Pour into a bowl or bowls and top with any of the suggested toppings, as desired.

Blackberry Honey Bowl

Blackberry and honey are two of my all-time favorite ingredients. They pair well with the pomegranate juice in this smoothie bowl.

Tip

Choose plump blackberries that are a deep shiny color and are at their peak season. To freeze them, arrange them in a single layer on a baking sheet, freeze until solid, then transfer to a sealable freezer bag. Store in the freezer for up to 9 months.

⅓ cup	unsweetened pomegranate juice	75 mL
1 tsp	liquid honey	5 mL
½	frozen banana, cut into pieces if necessary (see page 14)	½
1 cup	frozen blackberries	250 mL
1 tsp	ground flax seeds (flaxseed meal)	5 mL
¾ tsp	hemp seeds	3 mL
	Ice cubes (optional)	

SUGGESTED TOPPINGS

Sliced banana

Blackberries

Dried mulberries

Pomegranate seeds

Hemp seeds

Ground flax seeds (flaxseed meal)

1. In blender, combine pomegranate juice, honey, banana, blackberries, flax seeds and hemp seeds. Secure lid and blend (from low to high if using a variable-speed blender) until smooth. If a thicker consistency is desired, add ice, one cube at a time, and blend until smooth.

2. Pour into a bowl and top with any of the suggested toppings, as desired.

Purple Power

This smoothie has a beautiful purple color. You won't taste the kale at all.

Tip

Store honey in an airtight container in a dry place at room temperature for up to 1 year.

½ cup	plain Greek yogurt	125 mL
¼ cup	unsweetened pomegranate juice	60 mL
1 tsp	liquid honey	5 mL
½ cup	blackberries (fresh or frozen)	125 mL
½ cup	blueberries (fresh or frozen)	125 mL
1 cup	trimmed kale leaves	250 mL
	Ice cubes (optional)	

SUGGESTED TOPPINGS

Blueberries

Kitchen Sink Granola (page 218

Chia seeds

1. In blender, combine yogurt, pomegranate juice, honey, blackberries, blueberries and kale. Secure lid and blend (from low to high if using a variable-speed blender) until smooth. If a thicker consistency is desired, add ice, one cube at a time, and blend until smooth.

2. Pour into a bowl and top with any of the suggested toppings, as desired.

Mulberry Smoothie Bowl

Have you heard of mulberries? They are an excellent source of iron and vitamin C, and are a great option if you like dried fruit.

**MAKES
1 SERVING**

Tips

If you don't have a high-powered blender, soak the mulberries in the pomegranate juice for 15 to 20 minutes or until the berries begin to plump. Add the mulberries and juice to the blender and continue with the recipe.

Store dried mulberries in an airtight container to use in trail mix, granola, yogurt and baked-good recipes.

½ cup	vanilla-flavored Greek yogurt	125 mL
¼ cup	unsweetened pomegranate juice	60 mL
1 tsp	liquid honey	5 mL
1 cup	frozen blueberries	250 mL
¼ cup	dried mulberries (see tips, at left)	60 mL
1 tbsp	Kitchen Sink Granola (page 218)	15 mL
	Ice cubes (optional)	

SUGGESTED TOPPINGS

Blueberries

Dried mulberries

Pomegranate seeds

Kitchen Sink Granola

Hemp seeds

1. In blender, combine yogurt, pomegranate juice, honey, blueberries, mulberries and granola. Secure lid and blend (from low to high if using a variable-speed blender) until smooth. If a thicker consistency is desired, add ice, one cube at a time, and blend until smooth.

2. Pour into a bowl and top with any of the suggested toppings, as desired.

Strawberry Coconut Bowl

Even though my youngest son does not like coconut, he loved this recipe.

○○

MAKES 1 SERVING		

Tip

To toast coconut, spread it evenly on a baking sheet and bake in a preheated 350°F (180°C) oven, stirring occasionally, for 7 minutes or until light golden. You can also broil coconut for 2 minutes instead, but be sure to watch very carefully so it does not burn.

⅓ cup	unsweetened coconut milk beverage	75 mL
1 tsp	liquid honey	5 mL
½	frozen banana, cut into pieces if necessary (see page 14)	½
1 cup	frozen strawberries	250 mL
2 tbsp	toasted flaked coconut (see tip, at left)	30 mL
	Ice cubes (optional)	

SUGGESTED TOPPINGS

Sliced strawberries

Toasted flaked coconut

Coconut Granola (page 216)

1. In blender, combine coconut milk, honey, banana, strawberries and coconut. Secure lid and blend (from low to high if using a variable-speed blender) until smooth. If a thicker consistency is desired, add ice, one cube at a time, and blend until smooth.

2. Pour into a bowl and top with any of the suggested toppings, as desired.

Fiber Power

Prunes are a good source of potassium, iron and fiber and are great for digestive health.

Tip

Store prunes in an airtight container in a cool, dry place for up to 6 months. You can also refrigerate them for up to 9 months or freeze them for up to 1 year.

¼ cup	unsweetened apple juice	60 mL
½ tsp	ground flax seeds (flaxseed meal)	2 mL
1 cup	frozen strawberries	250 mL
¼ cup	prunes	60 mL
4	ice cubes	4

SUGGESTED TOPPINGS

Strawberries

Unsweetened shredded coconut

Chopped almonds

Sesame seeds

Hemp seeds

Ground flax seeds (flaxseed meal)

1. In blender, combine apple juice, flax seeds, strawberries, prunes and ice. Secure lid and blend (from low to high if using a variable-speed blender) until smooth.

2. Pour into a bowl and top with any of the suggested toppings, as desired.

Variation

Add 1 tbsp (15 mL) protein powder for additional thickness and protein. Blend it with the apple juice before adding the remaining ingredients.

Pick-Me-Up Bowl

Sprinkling flax seeds into this smoothie bowl will add omega-3 fatty acids and fiber to your diet.

Tips

If you are using a high-powered blender and don't have ground flax seeds, you can substitute whole flax seeds. Add them with the yogurt and protein powder.

You can use store-bought granola or any of the granola recipes in this book (pages 210–218) to top your smoothie bowl.

½ cup	strawberry-flavored Greek yogurt	125 mL
1	scoop protein powder	1
1 tsp	ground flax seeds (flaxseed meal)	5 mL
½ cup	frozen chopped pineapple	125 mL
½ cup	strawberries	125 mL
	Ice cubes (optional)	

SUGGESTED TOPPINGS

Chopped pineapple

Sliced strawberries

Granola

Chia seeds

1. In blender, combine yogurt and protein powder. Secure lid and blend (from low to high if using a variable-speed blender) until smooth. Add flax seeds, pineapple and strawberries; blend until smooth. If a thicker consistency is desired, add ice, one cube at a time, and blend until smooth.

2. Pour into a bowl and top with any of the suggested toppings, as desired.

Berry Healthy Bowl

This healthy smoothie bowl is full of my favorite ingredients, including pomegranate juice, berries, mango and banana.

MAKES 1 TO 2 SERVINGS

Tip

If you use frozen berries instead of fresh, omit the ice in this recipe.

¼ cup	unsweetened pomegranate juice	60 mL
1 tsp	liquid honey	5 mL
½ cup	frozen chopped mango	125 mL
1	ripe banana	1
¾ cup	strawberries	175 mL
¾ cup	blueberries	175 mL
4	ice cubes	4

SUGGESTED TOPPINGS

Strawberries

Blueberries

Classic Granola (page 210)

Chopped almonds

Golden raisins

1. In blender, combine pomegranate juice, honey, mango, banana, strawberries, blueberries and ice. Secure lid and blend (from low to high if using a variable-speed blender) until smooth.

2. Pour into a bowl or bowls and top with any of the suggested toppings, as desired.

Variation

Add 1 scoop of protein powder for additional thickness and protein. You will also need to add 2 tbsp (30 mL) water. Blend the protein powder with the pomegranate juice and honey before adding the remaining ingredients.

Feel Better Smoothie Bowl

This fruity blend will keep you feeling healthy and energetic.

**MAKES
1 SERVING**

Tips

If you use frozen berries instead of fresh, omit the ice in this recipe.

Store unripe avocados at room temperature and ripe ones that have been cut in an airtight container in the refrigerator. Sprinkle cut surfaces with lime or lemon juice to help prevent browning.

¼ cup	unsweetened pomegranate juice	60 mL
½	avocado	½
1 cup	trimmed baby spinach leaves	250 mL
⅓ cup	strawberries	75 mL
⅓ cup	blueberries	75 mL
4	ice cubes	4

SUGGESTED TOPPINGS

Sliced strawberries

Blueberries

Dried mulberries

Pomegranate seeds

1. In blender, combine pomegranate juice, avocado, spinach, strawberries, blueberries and ice. Secure lid and blend (from low to high if using a variable-speed blender) until smooth.

2. Pour into a bowl and top with any of the suggested toppings, as desired.

Awesome Anti-Inflammatory

Strawberries, blueberries and ginger are all known as anti-inflammatory ingredients, which means they can help reduce pain and swelling.

**MAKES
1 SERVING**

Tip

Use a vegetable peeler or a sharp paring knife to peel ginger.

⅓ cup	freshly squeezed orange juice	75 mL
1 tsp	liquid honey	5 mL
½ cup	strawberries (fresh or frozen)	125 mL
½ cup	blueberries (fresh or frozen)	125 mL
1 tsp	grated gingerroot	5 mL
	Ice cubes (optional)	

SUGGESTED TOPPINGS

Sliced strawberries

Blueberries

Hemp seeds

Ground flax seeds (flaxseed meal)

1. In blender, combine orange juice, honey, strawberries, blueberries and ginger. Secure lid and blend (from low to high if using a variable-speed blender) until smooth. If a thicker consistency is desired, add ice, one cube at a time, and blend until smooth.

2. Pour into a bowl and top with any of the suggested toppings, as desired.

Berry Banana Bowl

Strawberries are packed with fiber, vitamins and a high level of antioxidants. I love using them in smoothie bowls for color and, of course, great flavor.

**MAKES
1 SERVING**

Tip

If you use frozen strawberries instead of fresh, omit the ice in this recipe.

¾ cup	strawberry-flavored Greek yogurt	175 mL
¼ cup	water	60 mL
1	scoop protein powder	1
1	frozen banana, cut into pieces if necessary (see page 14)	1
¾ cup	strawberries	175 mL
4	ice cubes	4

SUGGESTED TOPPINGS

Sliced strawberries

Blueberries

Yogurt-covered raisins

Healthy Trail Mix (page 220)

1. In blender, combine yogurt, water and protein powder. Secure lid and blend (from low to high if using a variable-speed blender) until smooth. Add banana, strawberries and ice; blend until smooth.

2. Pour into a bowl and top with any of the suggested toppings, as desired.

Complete Breakfast Smoothie Bowl (page 22)

Breakfast To Go (page 25)

Superfood Smoothie Bowl (page 59)

Green Coconut Bowl (page 83)

Peanut Butter Cup (page 99)

Peach Paradise (page 114)

Berry Banana Bowl (page 144)

Pomegranate Berry Bowl (page 163)

Chilled Tiramisù (page 176)

Pomegranate Tea Bowl (page 179)

Upside-Down Apple Pie (page 190)

Chocolate Mint Smoothie Bowl (page 201)

Cherry Piña Colada

This twist on a piña colada features cherries and fabulous flavor.

Tips

If you use frozen cherries instead of fresh, you may not need any ice.

Start with the ripest fruit possible. If you're using fresh cherries and they aren't super-sweet, increase the honey in this recipe to 1 tbsp (15 mL).

Store unwashed cherries in an airtight plastic bag in the refrigerator for up to 5 days. Wash them right before using.

½ cup	plain Greek yogurt	125 mL
¼ cup	coconut water	60 mL
1 tsp	liquid honey	5 mL
1	frozen banana, cut into pieces if necessary (see page 14)	1
¾ cup	frozen chopped pineapple	175 mL
⅓ cup	cherries, pitted	75 mL
	Ice cubes (optional)	

SUGGESTED TOPPINGS

Sliced banana

Chopped pineapple

Pitted cherries

Unsweetened shredded coconut

Chia seeds

1. In blender, combine yogurt, coconut water, honey, banana, pineapple and cherries. Secure lid and blend (from low to high if using a variable-speed blender) until smooth. If a thicker consistency is desired, add ice, one cube at a time, and blend until smooth.

2. Pour into bowls and top with any of the suggested toppings, as desired.

Apricot Banana Bowl

Perfect for breakfast or an afternoon snack, this recipe is for apricot lovers. If fresh apricots are in season, add 1 cup (250 mL) chopped fresh apricots after the dried apricots.

Tip

If you don't have a high-powered blender, finely chop the dried apricots, then soak them in the milk for 15 to 20 minutes or until the apricots begin to plump. Add the apricots and milk to the blender and continue with the recipe.

½ cup	vanilla-flavored Greek yogurt	125 mL
⅓ cup	milk	75 mL
½	frozen banana, cut into pieces if necessary (see page 14)	½
⅔ cup	dried apricots (see tip, at left)	150 mL
	Ice cubes (optional)	

SUGGESTED TOPPINGS

Blueberries

Chopped dried apricots

Chopped walnuts

Green pumpkin seeds (pepitas)

Hemp seeds

1. In blender, combine yogurt, milk, banana and apricots. Secure lid and blend (from low to high if using a variable-speed blender) until smooth. If a thicker consistency is desired, add ice, one cube at a time, and blend until smooth.

2. Pour into a bowl and top with any of the suggested toppings, as desired.

Variations

For a dairy-free version, substitute ⅓ cup (75 mL) coconut water or unsweetened apple juice for the milk.

Add 1 tbsp (15 mL) protein powder for additional thickness and protein. Blend it with the liquids before adding the remaining ingredients.

Peaches and Cream

This is as good as it sounds — in the morning, as an afternoon treat or in the evening for dessert.

**MAKES
1 SERVING**

Tip

Use unsweetened vanilla-flavored almond milk for added vanilla flavor.

¼ cup	unsweetened almond milk	60 mL
1	scoop vanilla-flavored protein powder	1
1	frozen banana, cut into pieces if necessary (see page 14)	1
1½ cups	frozen sliced peaches	375 mL
	Ice cubes (optional)	

SUGGESTED TOPPINGS

Sliced banana

Sliced peaches

Unsweetened shredded coconut

Chia seeds

Ground flax seeds (flaxseed meal)

1. In blender, combine almond milk and protein powder. Secure lid and blend (from low to high if using a variable-speed blender) until smooth. Add banana and peaches; blend until smooth. If a thicker consistency is desired, add ice, one cube at a time, and blend until smooth.

2. Pour into a bowl and top with any of the suggested toppings, as desired.

Stone Fruit Smoothie Bowl

You don't need to peel the plums and nectarines for this recipe. Just wash them well, slice them and add them to the blender.

Tips

Any type of honey can be used in this recipe.

You can use store-bought granola or any of the granola recipes in this book (pages 210–218) to top your smoothie bowl.

¼ cup	unsweetened almond milk	60 mL
1 tsp	liquid honey	5 mL
1	frozen banana, cut into pieces if necessary (see page 14)	1
2	plums, sliced	2
2	nectarines, sliced	2
	Ice cubes (optional)	

SUGGESTED TOPPINGS

Sliced banana

Sliced plums

Sliced nectarines

Granola

Ground flax seeds (flaxseed meal)

1. In blender, combine almond milk, honey, banana, plums and nectarines. Secure lid and blend (from low to high if using a variable-speed blender) until smooth. If a thicker consistency is desired, add ice, one cube at a time, and blend until smooth.

2. Pour into bowls and top with any of the suggested toppings, as desired.

Creamy Cantaloupe Bowl

If you like cantaloupe, you'll love this recipe.

‹००›

**MAKES
1 SERVING**

Tips

Purchase precut
cantaloupe when you
have less time to make
smoothie bowls.

Store whole ripe
cantaloupes in the
refrigerator for up to
5 days.

Freeze leftover ripe
cantaloupe in an even
layer on a baking sheet.
When frozen, store in
airtight containers in
the freezer for up to
6 months.

¼ cup	milk	60 mL
½	frozen banana, cut into pieces if necessary (see page 14)	½
⅓ cup	frozen chopped pineapple	75 mL
1¼ cups	chopped cantaloupe	300 mL
2 tsp	unsweetened shredded coconut	10 mL
	Ice cubes (optional)	

SUGGESTED TOPPINGS

Sliced banana

Unsweetened shredded coconut

Chopped walnuts

Chia seeds

1. In blender, combine milk, banana, pineapple, cantaloupe and coconut. Secure lid and blend (from low to high if using a variable-speed blender) until smooth. If a thicker consistency is desired, add ice, one cube at a time, and blend until smooth.

2. Pour into a bowl and top with any of the suggested toppings, as desired.

Variation

Substitute ¼ cup (60 mL) unsweetened coconut milk beverage or coconut water for the milk.

Coco-Cantaloupe Bowl

Enjoy a taste of summer any time of year with this smoothie bowl, filled with frozen cantaloupe, pineapple and a hint of coconut.

Tip

Freeze chopped cantaloupe during the summer to have all year round. Arrange it in an even layer on a baking sheet. When frozen, store in airtight containers in the freezer for up to 6 months.

½ cup	coconut water	125 mL
1	frozen banana, cut into pieces if necessary (see page 14)	1
1½ cups	frozen chopped cantaloupe	375 mL
1 cup	frozen chopped pineapple	250 mL
	Ice cubes (optional)	

SUGGESTED TOPPINGS

Sliced banana
Chopped cantaloupe
Dried pineapple pieces
Unsweetened shredded coconut
Coconut Granola (page 216)
Chopped pecans
Ground flax seeds (flaxseed meal)

1. In blender, combine coconut water, banana, cantaloupe and pineapple. Secure lid and blend (from low to high if using a variable-speed blender) until smooth. If a thicker consistency is desired, add ice, one cube at a time, and blend until smooth.

2. Pour into bowls and top with any of the suggested toppings, as desired.

Watermelon Mint Bowl

Fresh mint and watermelon make a terrific, healthy combination.

Tips

When purchasing precut melon, look for bright-colored chunks that are firm and not mushy.

Use frozen watermelon or Watermelon Cubes (page 18) for a thicker smoothie consistency.

¼ cup	coconut water	60 mL
½	frozen banana, cut into pieces if necessary (see page 14)	½
1 cup	chopped seedless watermelon	250 mL
1 tbsp	fresh mint leaves	15 mL
4	ice cubes	4

SUGGESTED TOPPINGS

Sliced banana

Chopped watermelon

Chia seeds

Chopped fresh mint

1. In blender, combine coconut water, banana, watermelon, mint and ice. Secure lid and blend (from low to high if using a variable-speed blender) until smooth.

2. Pour into a bowl and top with any of the suggested toppings, as desired.

Variation

Substitute fresh basil for the mint.

Watermelon Strawberry Bowl

Watermelon smoothies are such a treat, and this version is also infused with strawberries and banana.

**MAKES
1 SERVING**

Tips

One pint (500 mL) of strawberries yields 1½ to 2 cups (375 to 500 mL) sliced or chopped.

You can use store-bought granola or any of the granola recipes in this book (pages 210–218) to top your smoothie bowl.

1 cup	chopped seedless watermelon	250 mL
1	scoop protein powder (optional)	1
½	frozen banana, cut into pieces if necessary (see page 14)	½
¾ cup	sliced strawberries	175 mL
4	ice cubes	4

SUGGESTED TOPPINGS

Chopped watermelon

Sliced banana

Sliced strawberries

Granola

Ground flax seeds (flaxseed meal)

1. In blender, combine watermelon and protein powder (if using). Secure lid and blend (from low to high if using a variable-speed blender) until smooth. Add banana, strawberries and ice; blend until smooth.

2. Pour into a bowl and top with any of the suggested toppings, as desired.

Grapefruit Watermelon Bowl

Watermelon and grapefruit both provide powerful antioxidants, and the two together create an amazing smoothie bowl.

**MAKES
1 SERVING**

Tip

Use frozen watermelon or Watermelon Cubes (page 18) for a thicker smoothie consistency.

1 cup	chopped seedless watermelon	250 mL
1 cup	chopped pink grapefruit	250 mL
½	frozen banana, cut into pieces if necessary (see page 14)	½
4	ice cubes	4

SUGGESTED TOPPINGS

Chopped watermelon

Sliced banana

Chopped almonds

Hemp seeds

Chia seeds

1. In blender, combine watermelon, grapefruit, banana and ice. Secure lid and blend (from low to high if using a variable-speed blender) until smooth.

2. Pour into a bowl and top with any of the suggested toppings, as desired.

Fruity Lime Bowl

This recipe has a powerful lime flavor that pairs nicely with the strawberries and mango.

**MAKES
2 SERVINGS**

Tip

One medium lime will yield about 1 tsp (5 mL) zest and 1½ tbsp (22 mL) juice.

1 cup	plain Greek yogurt	250 mL
½ tsp	grated lime zest	2 mL
1 tbsp	freshly squeezed lime juice	15 mL
½ cup	frozen chopped mango	125 mL
¾ cup	strawberries	175 mL
	Ice cubes (optional)	

SUGGESTED TOPPINGS

Sliced strawberries

Unsweetened shredded coconut

Grated lime zest

Chia seeds

Hemp seeds

1. In blender, combine yogurt, lime zest, lime juice, mango and strawberries. Secure lid and blend (from low to high if using a variable-speed blender) until smooth. If a thicker consistency is desired, add ice, one cube at a time, and blend until smooth.

2. Pour into bowls and top with any of the suggested toppings, as desired.

Dreamsicle

If you like the taste of a dreamsicle, you'll love this smoothie bowl creation.

**MAKES
1 SERVING**

Tips

Choose oranges that are firm and heavy for their size.

Feel free to omit the protein powder; simply add the fruit and ice with the orange juice and blend as directed.

¼ cup	freshly squeezed orange juice	60 mL
1 tbsp	vanilla-flavored protein powder	15 mL
1	frozen banana, cut into pieces if necessary (see page 14)	1
¾ cup	sliced oranges	175 mL
4	ice cubes	4

SUGGESTED TOPPINGS

Ground cinnamon

Sliced banana

Grated orange zest

Classic Granola (page 210)

Chopped pecans

1. In blender, combine orange juice and protein powder. Secure lid and blend (from low to high if using a variable-speed blender) until smooth. Add banana, oranges and ice; blend until smooth.

2. Pour into a bowl and top with any of the suggested toppings, as desired.

Banana Granola Bowl

My daughter, Leigh, created this recipe using her favorite smoothie bowl ingredients: banana and granola.

**MAKES
2 SERVINGS**

Tip
Be sure to blend this recipe well to make sure all the granola is chopped up and mixed evenly with the liquid.

¾ cup	unsweetened almond milk	175 mL
1 tsp	liquid honey	5 mL
1	scoop protein powder	1
2	frozen bananas, cut into pieces if necessary (see page 14)	2
1 cup	Classic Granola (page 210)	250 mL
4	ice cubes	4

SUGGESTED TOPPINGS
Sliced banana

Classic Granola

Chopped walnuts

Green pumpkin seeds (pepitas)

1. In a blender, combine almond milk, honey and protein powder. Secure lid and blend (from low to high if using a variable-speed blender) until smooth. Add bananas, granola and ice; blend until smooth.

2. Pour into bowls and top with any of the suggested toppings, as desired.

Dragon Fruit Berry Bowl

Frozen dragon fruit makes a very bright purple-colored smoothie bowl.

MAKES 1 SERVING

Tips

Purchase frozen dragon fruit at specialty grocery stores, health food stores or online.

Dragon fruit is also a great addition to desserts, salad dressings and beverages.

You can use store-bought granola or any of the granola recipes in this book (pages 210–218) to top your smoothie bowl.

¼ cup	unsweetened pomegranate juice	60 mL
½	frozen banana, cut into pieces if necessary (see page 14)	½
1 cup	frozen chopped dragon fruit	250 mL
½ cup	blueberries	125 mL
½ cup	strawberries	125 mL
	Ice cubes (optional)	

SUGGESTED TOPPINGS

Sliced strawberries

Blueberries

Sliced kiwifruit

Granola

Chopped almonds

Sunflower seeds

1. In blender, combine pomegranate juice, banana, dragon fruit, blueberries and strawberries. Secure lid and blend (from low to high if using a variable-speed blender) until smooth. If a thicker consistency is desired, add ice, one cube at a time, and blend until smooth.

2. Pour into a bowl and top with any of the suggested toppings, as desired.

Blue Kiwi Bowl

My family created this recipe when we were trying to use up blueberries and kiwi. It created a delicious and nutritious smoothie bowl!

MAKES 1 SERVING

Tips

If you can't find blueberry-flavored Greek yogurt, you can use regular blueberry-flavored yogurt or vanilla-flavored Greek yogurt.

Kiwifruit that are hard are not ripe yet.

If you prefer, you can use store-bought banana chips to top your smoothie bowl.

½ cup	blueberry-flavored Greek yogurt	125 mL
½	frozen banana, cut into pieces if necessary (see page 14)	½
½ tsp	chia seeds	2 mL
1	kiwifruit, peeled	1
½ cup	blueberries	125 mL
4	ice cubes	4

SUGGESTED TOPPINGS

Blueberries

Sliced strawberries

Grapes

Banana Chips (page 208)

Chia seeds

1. In blender, combine yogurt, banana, chia seeds, kiwi, blueberries and ice. Secure lid and blend (from low to high if using a variable-speed blender) until smooth.

2. Pour into a bowl and top with any of the suggested toppings, as desired.

Mango Tango

Mango, coconut water and kiwifruit are the stars of this smoothie bowl.

Tip

Store ripe mangos in a plastic bag in the refrigerator for up to 5 days. If you can't find ripe or frozen mango, you can use jarred or canned mangos, but they can often have added sugar, so be sure to read the ingredient list.

¼ cup	coconut water	60 mL
1	scoop protein powder	1
½	frozen banana, cut into pieces if necessary (see page 14)	½
1 cup	chopped mango (fresh or frozen)	250 mL
1	kiwifruit, peeled	1
4	ice cubes	4

SUGGESTED TOPPINGS

Sliced banana

Sliced kiwifruit

Chopped macadamia nuts

Chia seeds

1. In blender, combine coconut water and protein powder. Secure lid and blend (from low to high if using a variable-speed blender) until smooth. Add banana, mango, kiwi and ice; blend until smooth.

2. Pour into a bowl and top with any of the suggested toppings, as desired.

Tropical Blend

The color of this blend will remind you of an island sunset. Feel free to substitute frozen mixed fruit for the mango and pineapple.

**MAKES
2 SERVINGS**

Tip

Feel free to substitute your favorite milk — dairy or unsweetened nondairy — for the coconut water. Coconut milk beverage works great in this recipe.

1 cup	plain Greek yogurt	250 mL
¼ cup	coconut water	60 mL
½	frozen banana, cut into pieces if necessary (see page 14)	½
1 cup	frozen chopped mango	250 mL
1 cup	frozen chopped pineapple	250 mL
	Ice cubes (optional)	

SUGGESTED TOPPINGS

Sliced banana

Sliced kiwifruit

Goji berries

Unsweetened shredded coconut

1. In blender, combine yogurt, coconut water, banana, mango and pineapple. Secure lid and blend (from low to high if using a variable-speed blender) until smooth. If a thicker consistency is desired, add ice, one cube at a time, and blend until smooth.

2. Pour into bowls and top with any of the suggested toppings, as desired.

Papaya Mango Bowl

Papaya is rich in vitamins C and A, and low in calories. Its sweet taste combines wonderfully with the mango, banana and lime juice in this recipe.

**MAKES
1 SERVING**

Tips

If you can't find orange-mango juice, substitute regular orange juice.

You can use store-bought granola or any of the granola recipes in this book (pages 210–218) to top your smoothie bowl.

¼ cup	orange-mango juice	60 mL
2 tbsp	water	30 mL
2 tsp	freshly squeezed lime juice	10 mL
1 cup	frozen chopped papaya	250 mL
½ cup	frozen chopped mango	125 mL
½	ripe banana	½
	Ice cubes (optional)	

SUGGESTED TOPPINGS

Blueberries

Unsweetened flaked coconut

Granola

Hemp seeds

Chia seeds

Ground flax seeds (flaxseed meal)

1. In blender, combine orange-mango juice, water, lime juice, papaya, mango and banana. Secure lid and blend (from low to high if using a variable-speed blender) until smooth. If a thicker consistency is desired, add ice, one cube at a time, and blend until smooth.

2. Pour into a bowl and top with any of the suggested toppings, as desired.

Afternoon Delight

My daughter, Leigh, had this smoothie bowl after a full day of working out and said, "This is what I needed."

Tip

If fresh peaches and raspberries are not in season, you can use ½ cup (125 mL) each frozen sliced peaches and raspberries, but increase the water to ⅓ cup (75 mL) and use only 2 ice cubes, as needed, for thickness.

¼ cup	water	60 mL
½	frozen banana, cut into pieces if necessary (see page 14)	½
½ cup	frozen chopped pineapple	125 mL
1	peach, sliced	1
½ cup	raspberries	125 mL
4	ice cubes	4

SUGGESTED TOPPINGS

Sliced peach

Raspberries

Unsweetened shredded coconut

Hemp seeds

Ground flax seeds (flaxseed meal)

1. In blender, combine water, banana and pineapple. Secure lid and blend (from low to high if using a variable-speed blender) until smooth. Add peach, raspberries and ice; blend until smooth.

2. Pour into a bowl and top with any of the suggested toppings, as desired.

Pomegranate Berry Bowl

This recipe is filled with antioxidants from the pomegranate juice and berries.

Tips

Choose bright-colored raspberries that look plump and have no visible mold.

Add 1 tbsp (15 mL) protein powder for additional protein and thickness. Blend it with the pomegranate juice before adding the remaining ingredients.

¼ cup	unsweetened pomegranate juice	60 mL
½	frozen banana, cut into pieces if necessary (see page 14)	½
½ cup	blueberries	125 mL
¼ cup	raspberries	60 mL
4	ice cubes	4

SUGGESTED TOPPINGS

Sliced banana

Raspberries

Blueberries

Pomegranate seeds

Dried mulberries

Chia seeds

1. In blender, combine pomegranate juice, banana, blueberries, raspberries and ice. Secure lid and blend (from low to high if using a variable-speed blender) until smooth.

2. Pour into a bowl and top with any of the suggested toppings, as desired.

Chocolate, Avocado and Blueberry Bowl

This recipe is packed with superfood ingredients, including blueberries, avocado and cocoa powder.

MAKES 1 TO 2 SERVINGS

Tip

Sprinkle the cut sides of leftover avocado with lemon or lime juice and store in an airtight container in the refrigerator.

⅓ cup	unsweetened almond milk	75 mL
2 tsp	liquid honey	10 mL
1 tbsp	unsweetened cocoa powder	15 mL
1	frozen banana, cut into pieces if necessary (see page 14)	1
½	avocado	½
1 cup	blueberries	250 mL
	Ice cubes (optional)	

SUGGESTED TOPPINGS

Unsweetened cocoa powder

Sliced banana

Blueberries

Chopped pistachios

1. In blender, combine almond milk, honey, cocoa, banana, avocado and blueberries. Secure lid and blend (from low to high if using a variable-speed blender) until smooth. If a thicker consistency is desired, add ice, one cube at a time, and blend until smooth.

2. Pour into a bowl or bowls and top with any of the suggested toppings, as desired.

Beets and Berries

Beets may seem like a strange ingredient to add to a smoothie bowl, but they are sweet and pair wonderfully with the berries in this recipe. They also add great color!

MAKES 1 TO 2 SERVINGS

Tips

One lb (500 g) of raw beets will yield 1 cup (250 mL) chopped cooked beets.

Beets can be boiled, roasted or cooked in the microwave. However you choose to cook them, remove the skin (which comes off easily) after cooking.

You can use store-bought granola or any of the granola recipes in this book (pages 210–218) to top your smoothie bowl.

¼ cup	unsweetened apple juice	60 mL
½ cup	frozen blueberries	125 mL
½ cup	frozen strawberries	125 mL
⅓ cup	chopped cooked beets	75 mL
	Ice cubes (optional)	

SUGGESTED TOPPINGS
- Blueberries
- Strawberries
- Granola
- Chia seeds

1. In blender, combine apple juice, blueberries, strawberries and beets. Secure lid and blend (from low to high if using a variable-speed blender) until smooth. If a thicker consistency is desired, add ice, one cube at a time, and blend until smooth.

2. Pour into a bowl or bowls and top with any of the suggested toppings, as desired.

Cucumber Melon Bowl

Honeydew, grapes and cucumber are wonderful smoothie bowl ingredients that add sweetness and color to this recipe.

Tips

To freeze grapes so they won't stick together, place them on a baking sheet. Spread them out so they aren't touching each other and freeze until solid. Once frozen, store in an airtight container or freezer bag.

You can use store-bought granola or any of the granola recipes in this book (pages 210–218) to top your smoothie bowl.

¼ cup	unsweetened apple juice	60 mL
1 tsp	grated lime zest	5 mL
1 tsp	freshly squeezed lime juice	5 mL
1 cup	frozen green grapes	250 mL
1 cup	chopped honeydew melon	250 mL
⅓ cup	chopped seedless cucumber	75 mL
4	ice cubes	4

SUGGESTED TOPPINGS

Green grapes

Chopped honeydew melon

Grated lime zest

Granola

Chopped pecans

1. In blender, combine apple juice, lime zest, lime juice, grapes, melon, cucumber and ice. Secure lid and blend (from low to high if using a variable-speed blender) until smooth.

2. Pour into a bowl and top with any of the suggested toppings, as desired.

Pumpkin Pie Bowl

Pumpkin purée is a simple way to add a healthy orange vegetable to smoothie bowl recipes. All you need to do is open a can.

**MAKES
2 SERVINGS**

Tip

If you don't have pumpkin pie spice on hand, substitute ½ tsp (2 mL) additional ground cinnamon and ¼ tsp (1 mL) ground nutmeg.

½ cup	vanilla-flavored Greek yogurt	125 mL
¼ cup	unsweetened almond milk	60 mL
2 tsp	liquid honey	10 mL
½ tsp	pumpkin pie spice	2 mL
¼ tsp	ground cinnamon	1 mL
½ cup	pumpkin purée (not pie filling)	125 mL
4	ice cubes	4

SUGGESTED TOPPINGS

Dried cranberries

Unsweetened shredded coconut

Pumpkin Granola (page 217)

Spiced Pecans (page 221)

Sunflower seeds

Green pumpkin seeds (pepitas)

1. In blender, combine yogurt, almond milk, honey, pumpkin pie spice, cinnamon, pumpkin purée and ice. Secure lid and blend (from low to high if using a variable-speed blender) until smooth.

2. Pour into bowls and top with any of the suggested toppings, as desired.

Variation

Add 1 scoop of protein powder for additional protein and thickness. Blend it with the liquids before adding the remaining ingredients.

Pumpkin Carrot Bowl

My daughter tasted this and said, "OMG, this is so good."

Tip

Stock up on canned pumpkin purée during the fall, when it is more often readily available, and keep it on hand year-round.

⅓ cup	unsweetened almond milk	75 mL
2 tbsp	liquid honey	30 mL
1	frozen banana, cut into pieces if necessary (see page 14)	1
1 cup	chopped carrots	250 mL
1 cup	pumpkin purée (not pie filling)	250 mL
	Ice cubes (optional)	

SUGGESTED TOPPINGS

Ground cinnamon

Sliced banana

Sliced dates

Spiced Pecans (page 221)

Chopped walnuts

1. In blender, combine almond milk, honey, banana, carrots and pumpkin. Secure lid and blend (from low to high if using a variable-speed blender) until smooth. If a thicker consistency is desired, add ice, one cube at a time, and blend until smooth.

2. Pour into bowls and top with any of the suggested toppings, as desired.

Coffee and Tea Smoothie Bowls

Coconut Coffee Smoothie

If you like coconut and coffee, you'll love this one!

Tip

Wondering what else to do with turbinado sugar? I like to put it in my coffee or in oatmeal, but it also can be used in place of granulated sugar in cookie, muffin, cobbler and pie recipes. It also works great sprinkled on crème brûlée before using a blowtorch.

¼ cup	brewed coffee, chilled	60 mL
¼ cup	coconut milk	60 mL
2 tbsp	turbinado sugar	30 mL
½ tsp	ground cinnamon	2 mL
1	frozen banana, cut into pieces if necessary (see page 14)	1
4	ice cubes	4

SUGGESTED TOPPINGS

Sliced banana

Unsweetened shredded coconut

Dark chocolate–covered espresso beans

1. In blender, combine coffee, coconut milk, sugar, cinnamon, banana and ice. Secure lid and blend (from low to high if using a variable-speed blender) until smooth.

2. Pour into a bowl and top with any of the suggested toppings, as desired.

Espresso Smoothie Bowl

Coffee gives this recipe an extra kick and a bold flavor.

Tips

If you're not planning to use the brewed coffee right away, store it in an airtight container at room temperature or in the refrigerator.

If you prefer, you can use store-bought almond butter in place of homemade.

You can substitute your favorite chocolate milk for the chocolate soy milk in this recipe.

½ cup	sweetened chocolate-flavored soy milk	125 mL
¼ cup	brewed espresso, chilled	60 mL
1 cup	coffee-flavored frozen yogurt	250 mL
2 tsp	liquid honey	10 mL
1 tsp	unsweetened cocoa powder	5 mL
½	frozen banana, cut into pieces if necessary (see page 14)	½
2 tbsp	Homemade Almond Butter (page 226)	30 mL
4	ice cubes	4

SUGGESTED TOPPINGS

Unsweetened cocoa powder

Sliced banana

Dark chocolate–covered espresso beans

Chocolate chips

1. In blender, combine soy milk, coffee, frozen yogurt, honey, cocoa, banana, almond butter and ice. Secure lid and blend (from low to high if using a variable-speed blender) until smooth.

2. Pour into bowls and top with any of the suggested toppings, as desired.

Cappuccino Smoothie Bowl

This three-ingredient recipe will please all coffee lovers, whether you enjoy it in the morning, in the evening or as a dessert.

Tip

For the best brewed coffee, use the freshest coffee beans, make sure your coffee maker is clean and use filtered or bottled water.

⅓ cup	brewed coffee, chilled	75 mL
2 tbsp	unsweetened almond milk or milk	30 mL
1½ cups	coffee-flavored ice cream	375 mL
4	ice cubes	4

SUGGESTED TOPPINGS

Ground cinnamon

Dark chocolate–covered espresso beans

1. In blender, combine coffee, almond milk, ice cream and ice. Secure lid and blend (from low to high if using a variable-speed blender) until smooth.

2. Pour into bowls and top with any of the suggested toppings, as desired.

Frozen Mocha Smoothie Bowl

Smoothie bowls are a great way to use up leftover coffee. Chill it to make this recipe.

Tip

Store coffee beans in an airtight container at room temperature for up to 1 month.

¼ cup	brewed coffee, chilled	60 mL
¼ cup	chocolate milk	60 mL
1 cup	coffee-flavored frozen yogurt	250 mL
2 tsp	liquid honey	10 mL
2 tbsp	unsweetened cocoa powder	30 mL
4	ice cubes	4

SUGGESTED TOPPINGS

Unsweetened cocoa powder

Cacao nibs

Dark chocolate–covered espresso beans

1. In blender, combine coffee, chocolate milk, frozen yogurt, honey, cocoa and ice. Secure lid and blend (from low to high if using a variable-speed blender) until smooth.

2. Pour into a bowl or bowls and top with any of the suggested toppings, as desired.

Banana Mocha Madness

This recipe is breakfast in a bowl for coffee and banana lovers. Add protein powder for an additional protein boost (see variation, below).

Tips

If you have a pod-style coffee maker, purchase a mixed package of flavored coffee pods to create new coffee smoothie bowl recipes.

You can use store-bought granola or any of the granola recipes in this book (pages 210–218) to top your smoothie bowl.

⅓ cup	brewed hazelnut-flavored coffee, chilled	75 mL
2 tbsp	milk	30 mL
2 tsp	unsweetened cocoa powder	10 mL
1	frozen banana, cut into pieces if necessary (see page 14)	1
2 tsp	chocolate hazelnut spread	10 mL
4	ice cubes	4

SUGGESTED TOPPINGS

Unsweetened cocoa powder

Sliced banana

Granola

Cacao nibs

1. In blender, combine coffee, milk, cocoa, banana, chocolate hazelnut spread and ice. Secure lid and blend (from low to high if using a variable-speed blender) until smooth.

2. Pour into a bowl and top with any of the suggested toppings, as desired.

Variation

Add 1 scoop of vanilla-flavored protein powder for additional protein and thickness. Blend it with the liquids before adding the remaining ingredients.

Affogato Smoothie Bowl

The first time I tried an affogato was in Sausalito, California, and it was heavenly. Affogato is a traditional Italian espresso-based treat. It typically consists of a scoop of ice cream or gelato with a shot of hot espresso poured over the top. It makes a fun smoothie bowl recipe.

MAKES 2 SERVINGS

Tip

Make sure the coffee is completely chilled before preparing this recipe.

½ cup	espresso, chilled	125 mL
2 tbsp	unsweetened almond milk	30 mL
3 cups	coffee ice cream	750 mL
2 tsp	unsweetened cocoa powder	10 mL
	Ice cubes (optional)	

SUGGESTED TOPPINGS

Ground cinnamon

Unsweetened cocoa powder

Dark chocolate–covered espresso beans

Ground flax seeds (flaxseed meal)

1. In blender, combine coffee, almond milk, ice cream and cocoa. Secure lid and blend (from low to high if using a variable-speed blender) until smooth. If a thicker consistency is desired, add ice, one cube at a time, and blend until smooth.

2. Pour into bowls and top with any of the suggested toppings, as desired.

Chilled Tiramisù

This smoothie bowl tastes so good it could be dessert.

⅓ cup	strong brewed coffee, chilled	75 mL
1½ cups	vanilla-flavored frozen yogurt	375 mL
2 tsp	unsweetened cocoa powder	10 mL
2	graham cracker squares or lady fingers	2
2 tsp	chocolate hazelnut spread	10 mL
	Ice cubes (optional)	

MAKES 1 SERVING

Tips

Store chocolate hazelnut spread in a cool, dry place. It does not need to be refrigerated after opening.

Omit the graham crackers or lady fingers from the smoothie and just crumble them on top if you like a less crunchy smoothie texture.

SUGGESTED TOPPINGS

Unsweetened cocoa powder

Ground cinnamon

Crushed graham crackers

Chocolate shavings

1. In blender, combine coffee, frozen yogurt, cocoa, graham crackers and chocolate hazelnut spread. Secure lid and blend (from low to high if using a variable-speed blender) until smooth. If a thicker consistency is desired, add ice, one cube at a time, and blend until smooth.

2. Pour into a bowl and top with any of the suggested toppings, as desired.

Chamomile Berry Bowl

Chamomile tea is a traditional herbal tea that many people drink in the evening because it is reputed to help with insomnia. Combine it with frozen berries and chia seeds for a healthy smoothie bowl.

**MAKES
1 SERVING**

Tip

Make sure tea is completely steeped and chilled before adding it to smoothie bowls.

⅓ cup	brewed chamomile tea, chilled	75 mL
2 tsp	liquid honey	10 mL
1½ cups	frozen mixed berries	375 mL
1 tsp	chia seeds	5 mL
	Ice cubes (optional)	

SUGGESTED TOPPINGS

Berries

Sliced kiwifruit

Classic Granola (page 210)

Chia seeds

1. In blender, combine tea, honey, berries and chia seeds. Secure lid and blend (from low to high if using a variable-speed blender) until smooth. If a thicker consistency is desired, add ice, one cube at a time, and blend until smooth.

2. Pour into a bowl and top with any of the suggested toppings, as desired.

Cinnamon Tea Bowl

This recipe is comfort in a bowl, topped with fabulous extras.

Tip

When purchasing cinnamon-flavored tea leaves, smell them to make sure they are very fresh. Cinnamon tea pods are also sold in grocery stores and online.

⅓ cup	brewed cinnamon-flavored tea, chilled	75 mL
¼ cup	unsweetened almond milk	60 mL
2 tsp	liquid honey	10 mL
¾ tsp	ground cinnamon	3 mL
1	frozen banana, cut into pieces if necessary (see page 14)	1
4	ice cubes	4

SUGGESTED TOPPINGS

Ground cinnamon

Banana Chips (page 208)

Maple Cinnamon Granola (page 211)

Spiced Pecans (page 221)

Hemp seeds

1. In blender, combine tea, almond milk, honey, cinnamon, banana and ice. Secure lid and blend (from low to high if using a variable-speed blender) until smooth.

2. Pour into a bowl and top with any of the suggested toppings, as desired.

Pomegranate Tea Bowl

Pomegranate juice, tea and strawberries all contain antioxidants, so this smoothie bowl is healthy as well as delicious!

MAKES 1 TO 2 SERVINGS

Tip

If you can't find pomegranate-flavored tea, you can substitute any berry-flavored tea.

¼ cup	brewed pomegranate-flavored tea, chilled	60 mL
¼ cup	unsweetened pomegranate juice	60 mL
1 tbsp	liquid honey	15 mL
1½ cups	frozen strawberries	375 mL
	Ice cubes (optional)	

SUGGESTED TOPPINGS

Sliced strawberries

Pomegranate seeds

Goji berries

Easy Muesli (page 219)

Chia seeds

1. In blender, combine tea, pomegranate juice, honey and strawberries. Secure lid and blend (from low to high if using a variable-speed blender) until smooth. If a thicker consistency is desired, add ice, one cube at a time, and blend until smooth.

2. Pour into a bowl or bowls and top with any of the suggested toppings, as desired.

Green Tea Blueberry Bowl

Green tea has many health benefits. I love drinking it in the afternoon, but my favorite new thing is to make this smoothie bowl for a filling afternoon snack.

Tip

Store tea tightly sealed in a cool, dark place for up to 1 year.

⅓ cup	brewed green tea, chilled	75 mL
1 tsp	liquid honey	5 mL
1	frozen banana, cut into pieces if necessary (see page 14)	1
1 cup	frozen blueberries	250 mL
	Ice cubes (optional)	

SUGGESTED TOPPINGS

Sliced banana

Blueberries

Goji berries

1. In blender, combine tea, honey, banana and blueberries. Secure lid and blend (from low to high if using a variable-speed blender) until smooth. If a thicker consistency is desired, add ice, one cube at a time, and blend until smooth.

2. Pour into a bowl and top with any of the suggested toppings, as desired.

Honeydew Green Tea Bowl

Green tea and honeydew melon pair well in this yummy smoothie bowl.

Tip

For colder, tastier smoothie bowls, have all of your ingredients chopped and prepared before starting the recipe.

¼ cup	brewed green tea, chilled	60 mL
2 tsp	liquid honey	10 mL
1	frozen banana, cut into pieces if necessary (see page 14)	1
1½ cups	chopped honeydew melon	375 mL
4	ice cubes	4

SUGGESTED TOPPINGS

Sliced banana

Chopped honeydew melon

Blueberries

Goji berries

Unsweetened shredded coconut

Grated lime zest

1. In blender, combine tea, honey, banana, melon and ice. Secure lid and blend (from low to high if using a variable-speed blender) until smooth.

2. Pour into a bowl and top with any of the suggested toppings, as desired.

Watermelon Green Tea Bowl

Watermelon and green tea are both packed with health benefits. This filling recipe is a perfect way to cool down in the summertime heat.

½ cup	brewed green tea, chilled	125 mL
1 tbsp	liquid honey	15 mL
1	frozen banana, cut into pieces if necessary (see page 14)	1
2 cups	frozen chopped watermelon	500 mL
	Ice cubes (optional)	

MAKES 1 TO 2 SERVINGS

Tips

Substitute Watermelon Cubes (page 18) for the frozen watermelon and omit the ice.

If you don't have frozen watermelon, substitute 2 cups (500 mL) fresh seedless watermelon, reduce the green tea to 3 tbsp (45 mL) and add 1 scoop of protein powder and/or more ice. Blend protein powder with the liquids before adding the remaining ingredients.

SUGGESTED TOPPINGS

Sliced strawberries

Chopped seedless watermelon

Grated lime zest

1. In blender, combine tea, honey, banana and watermelon. Secure lid and blend (from low to high if using a variable-speed blender) until smooth. If a thicker consistency is desired, add ice, one cube at a time, and blend until smooth.

2. Pour into a bowl or bowls and top with any of the suggested toppings, as desired.

Green Tea and Lime Bowl

Green tea, lime, honey and avocado create a smoothie bowl with spectacular taste!

MAKES 1 TO 2 SERVINGS

Tip

Green tea does not require much time to steep — only 1 to 3 minutes. For the best flavor, don't oversteep it.

⅓ cup	brewed green tea, chilled	75 mL
1 tsp	grated lime zest	5 mL
1 tbsp	freshly squeezed lime juice	15 mL
2 tsp	liquid honey	10 mL
1	frozen banana, cut into pieces if necessary (see page 14)	1
1	avocado, cut into chunks	1
4	ice cubes	4

SUGGESTED TOPPINGS

Sliced banana

Unsweetened shredded coconut

Grated lime zest

Coconut Granola (page 216)

Hemp seeds

1. In blender, combine tea, lime zest, lime juice, honey, banana, avocado and ice. Secure lid and blend (from low to high if using a variable-speed blender) until smooth.

2. Pour into a bowl or bowls and top with any of the suggested toppings, as desired.

Mango Tango Tea Bowl

Green tea, blackberries, mango and banana create a thirst-quenching and very filling smoothie bowl.

Tip

To make the perfect cup of tea, use 1 heaping tsp (5 mL) of loose tea per 1 cup (250 mL) water, plus 1 tsp (5 mL) for the pot. If using tea bags, use one bag per 1 cup (250 mL).

⅓ cup	brewed green tea, chilled	75 mL
1	frozen banana, cut into pieces if necessary (see page 14)	1
¾ cup	frozen chopped mango	175 mL
1 cup	blackberries	250 mL
	Ice cubes (optional)	

SUGGESTED TOPPINGS

Sliced banana

Blackberries

Kitchen Sink Granola (page 218)

1. In blender, combine tea, banana, mango and blackberries. Secure lid and blend (from low to high if using a variable-speed blender) until smooth. If a thicker consistency is desired, add ice, one cube at a time, and blend until smooth.

2. Pour into a bowl and top with any of the suggested toppings, as desired.

Variation

If you prefer a sweeter smoothie bowl, add 1 to 2 tsp (5 to 10 mL) liquid honey after the tea.

Green Tea Pineapple Mojito

An iced green tea mojito in smoothie bowl form? Yes, please! For even more mint flavor, use mint ice cubes (see tip, below).

MAKES 1 SERVING

Tip

To make mint ice cubes, place finely chopped fresh mint in an ice cube tray, add water and freeze.

⅓ cup	brewed mint green tea, chilled	75 mL
1 tsp	grated lime zest	5 mL
1 tbsp	freshly squeezed lime juice	15 mL
2 tsp	liquid honey	10 mL
1¼ cups	frozen chopped pineapple	300 mL
2 tbsp	fresh mint leaves	30 mL
4	ice cubes	4

SUGGESTED TOPPINGS

Chopped pineapple

Grated lime zest

Chopped mint

1. In blender, combine tea, lime zest, lime juice, honey, pineapple, mint and ice. Secure lid and blend (from low to high if using a variable-speed blender) until smooth.

2. Pour into a bowl and top with any of the suggested toppings, as desired.

Peachy Tea Smoothie Bowl

Black tea is one of the most popular teas, but people tend to forget that it is also full of health benefits. It's wonderful here, with honey, peach and banana.

MAKES 1 TO 2 SERVINGS

Tips

If you use a frozen banana instead of a fresh one, you won't need to add any ice.

If fresh peaches are in season, use them in place of the frozen peaches, use a frozen banana and add more ice.

⅓ cup	brewed peach-flavored black tea, chilled	75 mL
1 tsp	liquid honey	5 mL
2 cups	frozen sliced peaches	500 mL
1	ripe banana	1
	Ice cubes (optional)	

SUGGESTED TOPPINGS

Sliced peaches
Sliced banana
Banana Chips (page 208)
Unsweetened shredded coconut
Classic Granola (page 210)

1. In blender, combine tea, honey, peaches and banana. Secure lid and blend (from low to high if using a variable-speed blender) until smooth. If a thicker consistency is desired, add ice, one cube at a time, and blend until smooth.

2. Pour into a bowl or bowls and top with any of the suggested toppings, as desired.

Vanilla Chai Smoothie Bowl

Chai spice is a mixture of dried spices that typically includes cinnamon, cardamom, ginger and cloves. These spices balance nicely with honey and vanilla frozen yogurt in this delectable smoothie bowl.

Tips

The best way to keep loose tea fresh is to store it in a stainless steel container in a cool, dark place for up to 1 year.

You can use store-bought granola or any of the granola recipes in this book (pages 210–218) to top your smoothie bowl.

⅓ cup	brewed chai tea, chilled	75 mL
2 cups	vanilla-flavored Greek frozen yogurt	500 mL
2 tsp	liquid honey	10 mL
1 tsp	vanilla extract	5 mL
½ tsp	ground cinnamon	2 mL
4	ice cubes	4

SUGGESTED TOPPINGS

Ground cinnamon

Granola

Trail Mix Cookies (page 225), crumbled

Chopped cashews

Green pumpkin seeds (pepitas)

Sunflower seeds

1. In blender, combine tea, frozen yogurt, honey, vanilla, cinnamon and ice. Secure lid and blend (from low to high if using a variable-speed blender) until smooth.

2. Pour into bowls and top with any of the suggested toppings, as desired.

Variation

Add 1 tbsp (15 mL) vanilla-flavored protein powder for additional protein and thickness. Blend it with the tea before adding the remaining ingredients.

Banana Chai Smoothie Bowl

Chai tea is great in this smoothie bowl, adding hints of cinnamon and ginger (and even fennel, in some blends).

**MAKES
1 SERVING**

Tip

If you prefer, you can use store-bought banana chips and granola to top your smoothie bowl.

⅓ cup	brewed chai tea, chilled	75 mL
2 tsp	liquid honey	10 mL
¼ tsp	ground cardamom	1 mL
1	frozen banana, cut into pieces if necessary (see page 14)	1
4	ice cubes	4

SUGGESTED TOPPINGS

Ground cardamom

Banana Chips (page 208)

Maple Cinnamon Granola (page 211)

1. In blender, combine tea, honey, cardamom, banana and ice. Secure lid and blend (from low to high if using a variable-speed blender) until smooth.

2. Pour into a bowl and top with any of the suggested toppings, as desired.

Dessert Bowls

Upside-Down Apple Pie

Apples are the star in this recipe. This is apple pie turned upside down in a smoothie bowl creation.

Tips

Use a Gala or Fuji apple for the sweetest apple taste.

You can use store-bought granola or any of the granola recipes in this book (pages 210–218) to top your smoothie bowl.

1	apple, peeled and cut into wedges	1
¼ cup	apple juice	60 mL
1 tsp	granulated sugar	5 mL
½ tsp	ground cinnamon	2 mL
¼ cup	milk	60 mL
1 cup	vanilla-flavored frozen yogurt	250 mL
4	graham crackers	4
4	ice cubes	4

SUGGESTED TOPPINGS

Ground cinnamon

Sliced peach

Granola

Crushed graham crackers

Spiced Pecans (page 221)

Caramel Sauce (page 231)

1. In a large skillet, combine apple and apple juice. Bring to a simmer over medium heat, then simmer for 5 minutes. Stir in sugar and cinnamon; simmer, stirring gently, for 3 minutes or until apples are softened. Drain and let cool completely.

2. In blender, combine milk, frozen yogurt, cooked apples, graham crackers and ice. Secure lid and blend (from low to high if using a variable-speed blender) until smooth.

3. Pour into a bowl and top with any of the suggested toppings, as desired.

Key Lime Pie

Did you know limes and avocados fight inflammation? Now you can feel good about eating this dessert smoothie bowl.

Tips

If you can't find Key lime–flavored yogurt, substitute vanilla-flavored yogurt and increase the lime zest to 2 tsp (10 mL).

To get the most juice out of a lime (or lemon), roll it against the counter beforehand.

1½ cups	Key lime–flavored yogurt	375 mL
3 tbsp	unsweetened almond milk	45 mL
1 tsp	grated lime zest	5 mL
1 tbsp	freshly squeezed lime juice	15 mL
1 tbsp	liquid honey	15 mL
1	frozen banana, cut into pieces if necessary (see page 14)	1
½	avocado	½
4	ice cubes	4

SUGGESTED TOPPINGS

Sliced banana

Grated lime zest

Crushed graham crackers

Whipped cream

1. In blender, combine yogurt, almond milk, lime zest, lime juice, honey, banana, avocado and ice. Secure lid and blend (from low to high if using a variable-speed blender) until smooth.

2. Pour into a bowl or bowls and top with any of the suggested toppings, as desired.

Blueberry Crumble

Blueberries have many health benefits and are filled with vitamin C. My daughter loves this combination of blueberries and bananas.

MAKES 1 TO 2 SERVINGS

Tips

You can use store-bought granola or any of the granola recipes in this book (pages 210–218) to top your smoothie bowl.

If you prefer your smoothie to have a less crunchy texture, omit the granola from the blender and just sprinkle it on top.

½ cup	blueberry-flavored yogurt	125 mL
¼ cup	milk or unsweetened almond milk	60 mL
2 tsp	liquid honey	10 mL
1	frozen banana, cut into pieces if necessary (see page 14)	1
2 tbsp	granola	30 mL
1 cup	blueberries	250 mL
4	ice cubes	4

SUGGESTED TOPPINGS

Sliced banana

Blueberries

Granola

Trail Mix Cookies (page 225), crumbled

1. In blender, combine yogurt, milk, honey, banana, granola, blueberries and ice. Secure lid and blend (from low to high if using a variable-speed blender) until smooth.

2. Pour into a bowl or bowls and top with any of the suggested toppings, as desired.

Shortcut Strawberry Shortcake

A smoothie bowl that tastes like strawberry shortcake: What else could you ask for? Serve in a mini sponge cake dessert shell, sold in the bakery section of grocery stores, for an added fun presentation.

**MAKES
2 SERVINGS**

Tip

For a dessert that is lower in calories and sugar, use vanilla-flavored nonfat Greek yogurt.

½ cup	vanilla-flavored frozen yogurt	125 mL
½	frozen banana, cut into pieces if necessary (see page 14)	½
2 cups	strawberries (fresh or frozen)	500 mL
	Ice cubes (optional)	

SUGGESTED TOPPINGS

Sliced banana

Sliced strawberries

Chopped lady fingers

1. In blender, combine frozen yogurt, banana and strawberries. Secure lid and blend (from low to high if using a variable-speed blender) until smooth. If a thicker consistency is desired, add ice, one cube at a time, and blend until smooth.

2. Pour into bowls and top with any of the suggested toppings, as desired.

Banana Split

My kids love making these, especially when they have company over.
Each creation is a work of art.

Tip

If you prefer, you can
use store-bought
raspberry sauce or
caramel sauce to top
your smoothie bowl.

½ cup	vanilla-flavored yogurt	125 mL
½ cup	chocolate-flavored yogurt	125 mL
½ cup	strawberry-flavored yogurt	125 mL
1	ripe banana	1
	Ice cubes (optional)	

SUGGESTED TOPPINGS

Sliced banana

Cherries

Chopped pecans

Chopped Spanish peanuts

Whipped cream

Raspberry Sauce (page 231)

Caramel Sauce (page 231)

1. In blender, combine vanilla, chocolate and strawberry
   yogurts and banana. Secure lid and blend (from low to
   high if using a variable-speed blender) until smooth. If
   a thicker consistency is desired, add ice, one cube at a
   time, and blend until smooth.

2. Pour into bowls and top with any of the suggested
   toppings, as desired.

Bananas Foster

Bananas Foster is my husband's favorite dessert, and we make it every year on his birthday. But he — and you — can enjoy this easy smoothie bowl version anytime.

MAKES 2 SERVINGS

Tips

If you prefer, you can substitute frozen yogurt (regular or Greek) for the ice cream, and your favorite nondairy milk for the milk.

Make sure that the Caramelized Bananas are completely cooled before adding them to the blender.

2 cups	vanilla ice cream	500 mL
2 tbsp	milk	30 mL
2	frozen bananas, cut into pieces if necessary (see page 14)	2
1 cup	Caramelized Bananas (page 226)	250 mL

SUGGESTED TOPPINGS

Ground cinnamon

Sliced banana

Crushed graham crackers

Spiced Pecans (page 221)

Caramel Sauce (page 231)

1. In blender, combine ice cream, milk, frozen bananas and Caramelized Bananas. Secure lid and blend (from low to high if using a variable-speed blender) until smooth.

2. Pour into bowls and top with any of the suggested toppings, as desired.

Banana Pudding

A twist on banana pudding, this recipe is a must-try! Bananas are full of vitamin B$_6$, vitamin C and potassium.

○○○

<table>
<tr><td>MAKES
2 SERVINGS</td><td>2 cups</td><td>vanilla ice cream</td><td>500 mL</td></tr>
<tr><td></td><td>2 tbsp</td><td>milk</td><td>30 mL</td></tr>
<tr><td></td><td>½ tsp</td><td>banana extract
(see tip, at left)</td><td>2 mL</td></tr>
<tr><td></td><td>2</td><td>frozen bananas, cut into pieces
if necessary (see page 14)</td><td>2</td></tr>
<tr><td></td><td></td><td>Ice cubes (optional)</td><td></td></tr>
</table>

Tips

If you don't have frozen bananas on hand, use ripe bananas and omit the milk. You will definitely need to add some ice.

If you can't find banana extract, you can substitute vanilla extract.

SUGGESTED TOPPINGS

Sliced banana

Vanilla wafers, crumbled

Whipped cream

1. In blender, combine ice cream, milk, banana extract and bananas. Secure lid and blend (from low to high if using a variable-speed blender) until smooth. If a thicker consistency is desired, add ice, one cube at a time, and blend until smooth.

2. Pour into bowls and top with any of the suggested toppings, as desired.

Variation

For a lighter version, use low-fat vanilla frozen yogurt in place of the ice cream and top with reduced-fat vanilla wafers.

Double Mango Bowl

My kids love this mango-filled smoothie bowl and ask for it all year round.

Tip

For easier, faster blending, defrost sorbet for 5 minutes at room temperature before adding it to your blender.

1½ cups	mango sorbet	375 mL
½ cup	vanilla-flavored Greek yogurt	125 mL
1 tsp	liquid honey	5 mL
1 cup	frozen chopped mango	250 mL
2 tbsp	unsweetened shredded coconut	30 mL
	Ice cubes (optional)	

SUGGESTED TOPPINGS

Raspberries

Unsweetened shredded coconut

Coconut Granola (page 216)

Hemp seeds

Ground flax seeds (flaxseed meal)

1. In blender, combine sorbet, yogurt, honey, mango and coconut. Secure lid and blend (from low to high if using a variable-speed blender) until smooth. If a thicker consistency is desired, add ice, one cube at a time, and blend until smooth.

2. Pour into bowls and top with any of the suggested toppings, as desired.

Variation

Double Peach Bowl: Substitute 1½ cups (375 mL) peach sorbet and 1 cup (250 mL) frozen sliced peaches for the mango.

Carrot Cake Smoothie Bowl

Made with traditional carrot cake ingredients, such as carrots, pineapple and cinnamon, this dessert bowl is a creative twist on a beloved favorite.

MAKES 1 SERVING

Tip

Carrots can be used in many smoothie recipes for added nutrition. Be sure to blend well to remove any chunks.

⅓ cup	sweetened vanilla-flavored soy milk	75 mL
1 tbsp	liquid honey	15 mL
½ tsp	ground cinnamon	2 mL
1	frozen banana, cut into pieces if necessary (see page 14)	1
1 cup	frozen chopped pineapple	250 mL
1 cup	chopped carrots	250 mL
4	ice cubes	4

SUGGESTED TOPPINGS

Ground cinnamon

Sliced banana

Chopped pineapple

Spiced Pecans (page 221)

Chopped walnuts

1. In blender, combine soy milk, honey, cinnamon, banana, pineapple, carrots and ice. Secure lid and blend (from low to high if using a variable-speed blender) until smooth.

2. Pour into a bowl and top with any of the suggested toppings, as desired.

Triple Chocolate Smoothie Bowl

No need to feel guilty when you enjoy this dessert: it's filled with three of the healthiest chocolate ingredients.

**MAKES
2 SERVINGS**

Tip

Look for cacao nibs at gourmet groceries, health food stores and online.

1 cup	sweetened chocolate-flavored soy milk	250 mL
2 cups	chocolate-flavored frozen Greek yogurt	500 mL
2 tbsp	unsweetened cocoa powder	30 mL
2 tsp	cacao nibs	10 mL
1	frozen banana, cut into pieces if necessary (see page 14)	1
4	ice cubes	4

SUGGESTED TOPPINGS

Sliced banana

Trail Mix Cookies (page 225), crumbled

Chopped peanuts

Cacao nibs

Chocolate shavings

1. In blender, combine soy milk, frozen yogurt, cocoa, cacao nibs, banana and ice. Secure lid and blend (from low to high if using a variable-speed blender) until smooth.

2. Pour into bowls and top with any of the suggested toppings, as desired.

Chocolate Banana

Satisfy your sweet tooth with this scrumptious mélange of chocolatey goodness.

Tips

Use the highest-quality vanilla extract in this recipe for the richest flavor.

You can use store-bought granola or any of the granola recipes in this book (pages 210–218) to top your smoothie bowl.

⅓ cup	chocolate milk	75 mL
2 cups	chocolate-flavored frozen Greek yogurt	500 mL
1 tsp	vanilla extract	5 mL
1	frozen banana, cut into pieces if necessary (see page 14)	1
	Ice cubes (optional)	

SUGGESTED TOPPINGS

Sliced banana

Granola

Best-Ever Chocolate Oat Cookies (page 223), crumbled

Graham crackers, crushed

Chopped almonds

Mini chocolate chips

Chocolate shavings

1. In blender, combine chocolate milk, frozen yogurt, vanilla and banana. Secure lid and blend (from low to high if using a variable-speed blender) until smooth. If a thicker consistency is desired, add ice, one cube at a time, and blend until smooth.

2. Pour into bowls and top with any of the suggested toppings, as desired.

Chocolate Mint Smoothie Bowl

This recipe is *so* good! With chocolate hazelnut spread, fresh mint and cocoa, this tastes like chocolate mint cookies in a bowl.

Tip

Be sure to blend this smoothie well for the creamiest texture.

⅓ cup	chocolate milk	75 mL
1¼ cups	chocolate-flavored frozen Greek yogurt	300 mL
1 tsp	unsweetened cocoa powder	5 mL
½	avocado	½
1 tbsp	chopped fresh mint	15 mL
1 tbsp	chocolate hazelnut spread	15 mL
4	ice cubes	4

SUGGESTED TOPPINGS

Chocolate mint cookies, crumbled

Chocolate chips

Chopped fresh mint

1. In blender, combine chocolate milk, frozen yogurt, cocoa, avocado, mint, chocolate hazelnut spread and ice. Secure lid and blend (from low to high if using a variable-speed blender) until smooth.

2. Pour into a bowl and top with any of the suggested toppings, as desired.

S'mores Smoothie Bowl

Your entire family will love this quick and easy recipe. Trust me — I know from experience.

Tip

When it comes to decorating this smoothie, the more marshmallows, the better. Who doesn't love s'mores?

¼ cup	milk	60 mL
2 cups	vanilla-flavored frozen yogurt	500 mL
2 tbsp	chocolate syrup	30 mL
1 tsp	unsweetened cocoa powder	5 mL
½ cup	mini marshmallows	125 mL
4	ice cubes	4

SUGGESTED TOPPINGS

Graham crackers, crushed
Chocolate chips
Mini marshmallows

1. In blender, combine milk, frozen yogurt, chocolate syrup, cocoa powder, marshmallows and ice. Secure lid and blend (from low to high if using a variable-speed blender) until smooth.

2. Pour into bowls and top with any of the suggested toppings, as desired.

Almond Butter Joy

With the natural goodness of almond butter, this healthy and delicious smoothie bowl dessert couldn't be easier.

Tips

If you prefer, use store-bought almond butter in place of the homemade.

Purchase unsalted raw almonds and store them in the refrigerator for up to 9 months or in the freezer for up to 1 year.

⅓ cup	unsweetened coconut milk beverage	75 mL
2 tbsp	chocolate syrup	30 mL
2 tsp	unsweetened cocoa powder	10 mL
1	frozen banana, cut into pieces if necessary (see page 14)	1
½ cup	Homemade Almond Butter (page 226)	125 mL
2 tbsp	sweetened shredded coconut	30 mL
4	ice cubes	4

SUGGESTED TOPPINGS

Unsweetened cocoa powder

Sliced banana

Sweetened shredded coconut

Chopped almonds

1. In blender, combine coconut milk, chocolate syrup, cocoa, banana, almond butter, coconut and ice. Secure lid and blend (from low to high if using a variable-speed blender) until smooth.

2. Pour into a bowl or bowls and top with any of the suggested toppings, as desired.

Candy Bar Smoothie Bowl

Do you like peanut-butter-and-chocolate candy bars? If so, this recipe is for you. It also makes a fun dessert idea for a birthday party.

MAKES 2 SERVINGS

Tips

If you do not have a high-powered blender, chop the candy bars into small pieces before blending them.

Substitute any of your favorite candy bars in this recipe.

½ cup	unsweetened almond milk	125 mL
2 cups	vanilla- or chocolate-flavored frozen yogurt or ice cream	500 mL
½ cup	peanut butter	125 mL
3	snack-size peanut butter chocolate candy bars (or 1 regular-size)	3
2	snack-size milk chocolate candy bar (or 1 regular-size)	2
4	ice cubes	4

SUGGESTED TOPPINGS

Best-Ever Chocolate Oat Cookies (page 223), crumbled

Chopped peanuts

Candy bar pieces

Caramel Sauce (page 231)

1. In blender, combine almond milk, frozen yogurt, peanut butter, candy bars and ice. Secure lid and blend (from low to high if using a variable-speed blender) until smooth.

2. Pour into bowls and top with any of the suggested toppings, as desired.

Cookies and Cream Bowl

This is cookies and cream heaven in a bowl — one of my son Zachary's all-time favorites.

Tip

Store leftover cookies in a sealable plastic bag in a cool, dry place for optimum freshness.

1 cup	vanilla ice cream or vanilla-flavored frozen yogurt	250 mL
2 tbsp	milk	30 mL
4	cream-filled chocolate sandwich cookies (such as Oreos)	4
4	ice cubes	4

SUGGESTED TOPPING

Crushed cream-filled chocolate sandwich cookies

1. In blender, combine ice cream, milk, cookies and ice. Secure lid and blend (from low to high if using a variable-speed blender) until smooth.

2. Pour into a bowl or bowls and top with crushed cookies.

Variation

Substitute mint-cream-filled chocolate sandwich cookies.

Chocolate Chip and Oat Bowl

I admit it: I have a sweet spot for chocolate chip oatmeal cookies. This three-ingredient recipe is guiltless pleasure after a hard day of work and working out.

MAKES 1 TO 2 SERVINGS

Tip

To make this recipe lower in calories and sugar, use nonfat plain Greek yogurt, omit the milk and add more ice, one cube at a time, blending until the desired consistency is achieved.

1 cup	vanilla-flavored frozen Greek yogurt	250 mL
2 tbsp	milk	30 mL
4	Best-Ever Chocolate Oat Cookies (page 223), crumbled	4
4	ice cubes	4

SUGGESTED TOPPINGS

Best-Ever Chocolate Oat Cookies, crumbled

Mini chocolate chips

1. In blender, combine frozen yogurt, milk, cookies and ice. Secure lid and blend (from low to high if using a variable-speed blender) until smooth.

2. Pour into a bowl or bowls and top with the suggested toppings, as desired.

Toppings

Apple Chips

I love this fast apple chip recipe, which uses the microwave instead of the oven, saving 2 hours.

**MAKES ABOUT
1 CUP (250 ML)**

Tip

Use Braeburn, Fuji, Honeycrisp or Golden Delicious apples for a sweet chip.

- **Microwave-safe plate, lined with parchment paper**

2	apples	2
½ tsp	ground cinnamon	2 mL

1. Core apples, cut in half, then cut lengthwise into ⅛-inch (3 mm) slices. Working in batches as necessary, arrange apple slices in a single layer on prepared plate. Sprinkle with cinnamon.

2. Microwave on High for 4 to 5 minutes or until edges of apples start to curl up. Turn slices over and microwave on High for 30 to 60 seconds or until edges are crisp. Remove from microwave and let stand for 10 minutes, until dried.

3. Store in an airtight container at room temperature for up to 3 days.

Banana Chips

Try making your own banana chips at home — it's easy!

**MAKES
ABOUT ½ CUP
(125 ML)**

Tips

Be sure not to use too much lemon juice or your chips will be slimy.

Be sure to cook these on low and slow heat so they dry completely and become crispy.

- **Preheat oven to 200°F (100°C)**
- **Baking sheet, sprayed with nonstick cooking spray**

4	ripe bananas, cut crosswise into ¼-inch (0.5 cm) slices	2
½ cup	freshly squeezed lemon juice	125 mL

1. Dip banana slices in lemon juice, shaking off excess. Arrange in a single layer on prepared baking sheet.

2. Bake in preheated oven for 2 to 2½ hours, turning once, until golden brown and crispy. Let cool completely on pan.

3. Store in an airtight container at room temperature for up to 1 week.

Kale Chips

These surprisingly delectable chips are fun as a topping for green smoothie bowls. Serve leftovers for a snack or appetizer.

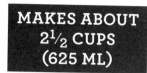

**MAKES ABOUT
2½ CUPS
(625 ML)**

Tips

Be sure to wash and dry kale leaves thoroughly and remove the stems before use.

You can double the recipe and bake in batches for extra chips.

- Preheat oven to 450°F (230°C)
- Baking sheet, lined with foil and lightly greased

3 cups	trimmed kale leaves	750 mL
2 tbsp	olive oil	30 mL
¼ tsp	sea salt	1 mL
¼ tsp	freshly ground black pepper	1 mL

1. On prepared baking sheet, toss kale with oil, salt and pepper. Spread in a single layer.

2. Bake in preheated oven for 6 minutes. Toss gently, reduce oven temperature to 300°F (150°C) and bake for 6 minutes or until crisp. Let cool on pan for 5 minutes.

3. Store in an airtight container at room temperature for up to 2 weeks.

Classic Granola

This simple granola recipe is so easy and fabulous. Feel free to add any of your favorite ingredients, such as flax seeds, sunflower seeds or hemp seeds.

**MAKES ABOUT
3½ CUPS
(875 ML)**

Tip

For homemade granola, I typically prefer large-flake (old-fashioned) rolled oats over quick-cooking oats.

- Preheat oven to 300°F (150°C)
- Baking sheet, lined with parchment paper

2 cups	large-flake (old-fashioned) rolled oats	500 mL
¾ cup	chopped nuts (any type)	175 mL
¼ cup	liquid honey	60 mL
2 tbsp	melted virgin coconut oil	30 mL
¾ cup	dried fruit (any type)	175 mL

1. In a large bowl, combine oats, nuts, honey and oil, stirring to coat. Spread in an even layer on prepared baking sheet, pressing gently to flatten.

2. Bake in preheated oven for 30 minutes, stirring halfway through, until golden brown. Remove from oven and stir in dried fruit. Let cool completely on pan on a wire rack.

3. Store in an airtight container at room temperature for up to 1 week.

Maple Cinnamon Granola

This recipe is one of my daughter's favorites. It has just the right blend of cinnamon, maple and vanilla.

Tips

When purchasing vanilla, choose real vanilla extract. My favorite is Mexican vanilla, which can be found at specialty grocery or spice stores. It has great flavor!

Feel free to use liquid coconut oil in place of the melted virgin coconut oil.

- Preheat oven to 325°F (160°C)
- Large baking sheet, lined with parchment paper

4 cups	large-flake (old-fashioned) rolled oats	1 L
1/3 cup	packed light brown sugar	75 mL
2 tsp	ground cinnamon	10 mL
1/2 cup	pure maple syrup	125 mL
1/3 cup	melted virgin coconut oil	75 mL
2 tsp	vanilla extract	10 mL

1. In a large bowl, combine oats, brown sugar, cinnamon, maple syrup, coconut oil and vanilla, stirring to coat. Spread in an even layer on prepared baking sheet, pressing gently to flatten.

2. Bake in preheated oven for 15 to 20 minutes, stirring halfway through, until golden brown. Let cool completely on pan on a wire rack.

3. Store in an airtight container at room temperature for up to 2 weeks.

Peanut Butter Granola

I love this granola sprinkled on any smoothie bowl made with peanut butter. It also makes a great healthy snack or breakfast served on top of yogurt or mixed with another cereal.

MAKES ABOUT 2 CUPS (500 ML)

Tip

Use a spatula to gently press the granola down into an even layer on the baking sheet. This will help it bake more evenly.

- **Preheat oven to 325°F (160°C)**
- **Baking sheet, lined with parchment paper**

1 tbsp	packed brown sugar	15 mL
¼ cup	creamy peanut butter	60 mL
¼ cup	liquid honey	60 mL
1 tsp	ground cinnamon	5 mL
½ tsp	vanilla extract	2 mL
2 cups	large-flake (old-fashioned) rolled oats	500 mL

1. In a large, microwave-safe bowl, combine brown sugar, peanut butter and honey. Microwave on High for 30 seconds, until melted.

2. Stir in cinnamon and vanilla. Stir in oats until well coated. Spread in an even layer on prepared baking sheet, pressing gently to flatten.

3. Bake in preheated oven for 18 to 20 minutes, stirring every 5 minutes, until golden brown. Let cool completely on pan on a wire rack.

4. Store in an airtight container at room temperature for up to 1 week.

Pecan Granola

If you're a pecan lover, this recipe is for you. Sprinkle it on smoothie bowls or enjoy it as a snack or with yogurt for breakfast.

Tips

Liquid honey can be substituted for the maple syrup.

If you prefer, you can use melted virgin coconut oil in place of the vegetable oil.

Use tongs to gently toss the granola occasionally while baking.

- **Preheat oven to 325°F (160°C)**
- **Large baking sheet, lined with parchment paper**

⅓ cup	packed light brown sugar	75 mL
2 tsp	ground cinnamon	10 mL
½ tsp	salt	2 mL
⅓ cup	pure maple syrup	75 mL
4 tsp	vanilla extract	20 mL
½ cup	vegetable oil	125 mL
5 cups	large-flake (old-fashioned) rolled oats	1.25 L
2 cups	chopped pecans	500 mL
2 cups	dried cranberries or cherries	500 mL

1. In a large bowl, whisk together brown sugar, cinnamon, salt, maple syrup and vanilla. Whisk in oil. Stir in oats and pecans until evenly coated. Spread in an even layer on prepared baking sheet, pressing gently to flatten.

2. Bake in preheated oven for 30 minutes, tossing gently occasionally, until lightly browned. Remove from oven and stir in cranberries. Let cool completely on pan on a wire rack.

3. Store in an airtight container at room temperature for up to 2 weeks.

Cashew and Cranberry Granola

This cashew granola is a fabulous topping for just about any smoothie bowl.

Tip

Substitute your favorite dried fruit for the dried cranberries.

- **Preheat oven to 350°F (180°C)**
- **Large baking sheet, lined with parchment paper**

1 cup	large-flake (old-fashioned) rolled oats	250 mL
⅓ cup	chopped cashews	75 mL
¼ cup	chopped walnuts	60 mL
1 tsp	ground flax seeds (flaxseed meal)	5 mL
¼ cup	pure maple syrup	60 mL
1 tbsp	melted virgin coconut oil	15 mL
1 tsp	ground cinnamon	5 mL
½ tsp	salt	2 mL
⅓ cup	dried cranberries, roughly chopped	75 mL

1. In a large bowl, combine oats, cashews, walnuts and flax seeds.

2. In a small microwave-safe bowl, combine maple syrup and coconut oil. Microwave on High for 20 seconds. Stir in cinnamon and salt.

3. Pour syrup mixture over oat mixture and stir until evenly coated. Spread in an even layer on prepared baking sheet, pressing gently to flatten.

4. Bake in preheated oven for 10 minutes. Stir in cranberries and bake for 5 minutes or until granola is golden brown. Let cool completely on pan on a wire rack.

5. Store in an airtight container at room temperature for up to 2 weeks.

Cherry Almond Granola

This homemade granola is chock-full of oats, nuts, seeds and dried cherries.

Tip

If you don't have flax seeds or hemp seeds on hand, feel free to add more nuts or pumpkin or sunflower seeds.

- Preheat oven to 325°F (160°C)
- Large baking sheet, lined with parchment paper

2 cups	large-flake (old-fashioned) rolled oats	500 mL
½ cup	unsweetened flaked coconut	125 mL
½ cup	chopped almonds	125 mL
2 tbsp	unsalted sunflower seeds	30 mL
1 tbsp	green pumpkin seeds (pepitas)	15 mL
1 tbsp	ground flax seeds (flaxseed meal)	15 mL
1 tbsp	hemp seeds	15 mL
3 tbsp	melted virgin coconut oil	45 mL
2 tbsp	pure maple syrup	30 mL
1 tsp	vanilla extract	5 mL
½ tsp	ground cinnamon	2 mL
¾ cup	chopped dried cherries	175 mL

1. In a large bowl, combine oats, coconut, almonds, sunflower seeds, pumpkin seeds, flax seeds and hemp seeds.

2. In a small bowl, combine coconut oil, maple syrup, vanilla and cinnamon, stirring well. Pour over oat mixture and stir until evenly coated. Spread in an even layer on prepared baking sheet, pressing gently to flatten.

3. Bake in preheated oven for 20 minutes, stirring after 10 minutes, until golden brown. Remove from oven and stir in cherries. Let cool completely on pan on a wire rack.

4. Store in an airtight container at room temperature for up to 2 weeks.

Coconut Granola

If you're a fan of coconut, you'll love this granola with standout coconut flavor and crunch.

Tips

You can use almonds or any other type of nuts in place of the walnuts and/or pecans.

Feel free to use liquid coconut oil in place of the softened virgin coconut oil.

- **Preheat oven to 300°F (150°C)**
- **Large baking sheet, lined with parchment paper**

3 cups	large-flake (old-fashioned) rolled oats	750 mL
½ cup	chopped pecans	125 mL
½ cup	chopped walnuts	125 mL
½ cup	unsalted sunflower seeds	125 mL
½ cup	sweetened shredded coconut	125 mL
¼ cup	ground flax seeds (flaxseed meal)	60 mL
1 tsp	ground cinnamon	5 mL
¼ tsp	salt	1 mL
½ cup	pure maple syrup	125 mL
½ cup	softened virgin coconut oil	125 mL
1 tbsp	vanilla extract	15 mL
1	large egg white, beaten	1
1 cup	dried fruit (optional)	250 mL

1. In a large bowl, combine oats, pecans, walnuts, sunflower seeds, coconut, flax seeds, cinnamon and salt.

2. In a small, heavy saucepan, combine maple syrup, coconut oil and vanilla. Heat over low heat, stirring, for 2 minutes. Add egg white, mixing well.

3. Pour syrup mixture over oat mixture and stir until evenly coated. Spread in an even layer on prepared baking sheet, pressing gently to flatten.

4. Bake in preheated oven for 40 minutes, stirring every 10 minutes, until lightly browned. Remove from oven and stir in dried fruit (if using). Let cool completely on pan on a wire rack.

5. Store in an airtight container at room temperature for up to 1 week.

Pumpkin Granola

This fabulous granola adds a slight taste of pumpkin when used to top smoothie bowls. Everyone in my family loves it.

Tip

Be sure to not overcook granola. Granola will often continue to bake when you remove it from the oven.

• Preheat oven to 325°F (160°C)
• Large baking sheet, lined with parchment paper

3 cups	large-flake (old-fashioned) rolled oats	750 mL
¾ cup	chopped pecans	175 mL
¼ cup	ground flax seeds (flaxseed meal)	60 mL
2 tbsp	green pumpkin seeds (pepitas)	30 mL
2 tbsp	packed brown sugar	30 mL
1 tsp	pumpkin pie spice	5 mL
¼ tsp	ground cinnamon	1 mL
¼ tsp	salt	1 mL
¼ cup	pure maple syrup	60 mL
¼ cup	softened virgin coconut oil	60 mL
¼ cup	pumpkin purée (not pie filling)	60 mL
½ cup	dried cranberries (optional)	125 mL

1. In a large bowl, combine oats, pecans, flax seeds, pumpkin seeds, brown sugar, pumpkin pie spice, cinnamon and salt.

2. In a small saucepan, combine maple syrup, coconut oil and pumpkin purée. Heat over low heat, whisking constantly, for 5 minutes or until well combined.

3. Pour syrup mixture over oat mixture and stir until evenly coated. Spread in an even layer on prepared baking sheet, pressing gently to flatten.

4. Bake in preheated oven for 30 minutes, stirring every 10 minutes, until lightly browned. Remove from oven and stir in cranberries (if using). Let cool completely on pan on a wire rack.

5. Store in an airtight container at room temperature for up to 1 week.

Kitchen Sink Granola

I threw everything into this one — and it's my top go-to granola recipe.

Tip

Add dried fruit after baking; otherwise, it will get crispy.

- **Preheat oven to 325°F (160°C)**
- **Large baking sheet, lined with parchment paper**

2½ cups	large-flake (old-fashioned) oats	625 mL
1 cup	chopped pecans	250 mL
½ cup	chopped walnuts	125 mL
½ cup	sunflower seeds	125 mL
2 tbsp	pistachios	30 mL
2 tbsp	unsweetened shredded coconut	30 mL
1 tbsp	ground flax seeds (flaxseed meal)	15 mL
1 tbsp	hemp seeds	15 mL
¼ cup	softened virgin coconut oil	60 mL
⅓ cup	liquid honey	75 mL
¾ cup	dried fruit (chopped if bigger than raisins)	175 mL

1. In a large bowl, combine oats, pecans, walnuts, sunflower seeds, pistachios, coconut, flax seeds and hemp seeds.

2. In a medium saucepan, combine coconut oil and honey. Bring to a boil over medium heat, stirring occasionally.

3. Immediately pour oil mixture over oat mixture and stir until evenly coated. Spread in an even layer on prepared baking sheet, pressing gently to flatten.

4. Bake in preheated oven for 20 to 25 minutes, stirring every 5 minutes, until golden brown. Remove from oven and stir in dried fruit. Let cool completely on pan on a wire rack.

5. Store in an airtight container at room temperature for up to 1 week.

Easy Muesli

My kids are constantly snacking on this fantastic healthy mix.

Tip

If you want to warm the muesli, stir in the desired amount of water or milk and microwave on High for 1 minute or cook in a saucepan over low heat for 5 minutes.

- Preheat oven to 350°F (180°C)
- Large baking sheet, lined with parchment paper

2½ cups	ready-to-eat whole-grain flaked cereal	625 mL
1½ cups	large-flake (old-fashioned) or quick-cooking rolled oats	375 mL
1½ cups	chopped mixed dried fruit	375 mL
½ cup	chopped mixed nuts	125 mL
1 tbsp	sunflower seeds	15 mL

1. Spread whole-grain flakes and oats in an even layer on prepared baking sheet. Bake in preheated oven for 6 to 8 minutes or until lightly toasted. Let cool completely on pan on a wire rack.

2. Stir in dried fruit, nuts and sunflower seeds.

3. Store in an airtight container for up to 3 weeks.

Healthy Trail Mix

This easy, slightly sweet trail mix is wonderful on top of any smoothie bowl.

Tip

Toast coconut in a preheated 350°F (180°C) oven for 6 to 8 minutes (or under the broiler for 2 minutes), until lightly browned.

1 cup	almonds	250 mL
½ cup	chopped walnuts	125 mL
¼ cup	green pumpkin seeds (pepitas)	60 mL
¼ cup	dried goji berries	60 mL
2 tbsp	unsweetened coconut flakes, toasted (see tip, at left)	30 mL

1. In a large bowl, combine almonds, walnuts, pumpkin seeds, goji berries and coconut.

2. Store in an airtight container in the refrigerator for up to 1 week.

Variation

Substitute dried cherries, raisins or chopped dried pineapple or apricots for the goji berries.

Spiced Pecans

These spicy nuts are great as a topping on any recipe in this book or served alongside coffee or tea.

MAKES ABOUT 4 CUPS (1 L)

Tip

Purchase pecans in bulk for the best prices.

- Preheat oven to 300°F (150°C)
- Baking sheet, sprayed with nonstick cooking spray

1 cup	granulated sugar	250 mL
2 tsp	pumpkin pie spice	10 mL
1	large egg white	1
1 tsp	water	5 mL
4 cups	pecan halves	1 L

1. In a large bowl, combine sugar and pumpkin pie spice, mixing well. Using a fork, beat in egg white and water. Add pecans and toss to coat. Spread in an even layer on prepared baking sheet.

2. Bake in preheated oven for 25 minutes, stirring halfway through. Let cool completely on pan on a wire rack. Break into bite-size pieces.

3. Store in an airtight container in a cool, dry place for up to 1 week.

No-Bake Flaxseed Bars

This recipe from my dear friend Nancy is the best! Crumble the bars to top any smoothie bowl.

MAKES 12 TO 18 BARS

Tip

Almond butter may be substituted for the peanut butter.

- **8-inch (20 cm) baking pan, lined with foil and lightly greased**

1 cup	large-flake (old-fashioned) rolled oats	250 mL
3 tbsp	ground flax seeds (flaxseed meal)	45 mL
½ cup	crunchy peanut butter	125 mL
¼ cup	liquid honey	60 mL
1 tsp	vanilla extract	5 mL
½ cup	dark chocolate chips	125 mL
½ cup	unsweetened shredded coconut (optional)	125 mL

1. In a large bowl, combine oats, flax seeds, peanut butter, honey and vanilla, mixing well. Gently stir in chocolate chips and coconut (if using). Press firmly into prepared pan.

2. Cover and refrigerate for at least 4 hours, until firm. Lift bars from pan using foil and transfer to a cutting board; cut into bars.

3. Store bars in an airtight container in the refrigerator for up to 1 week.

Variation

No-Bake Flaxseed Balls: Instead of pressing the mixture into a pan, use moistened hands to form it into bite-sized balls. If desired, roll the balls in finely chopped flaked coconut. Place on a baking sheet, cover and refrigerate until firm.

Best-Ever Chocolate Oat Cookies

My friend Nancy shared this recipe with me. She says these are the best chocolate chip cookies she has ever made.

MAKES 48 COOKIES

Tips

Be sure not to overbake these cookies, as they will continue to cook when you remove them from the oven. Remove them when they are lightly browned around the edges.

The chocolate chips can be omitted if you prefer plain oatmeal cookies.

Store cookies in an airtight container at room temperature for up to 1 week.

• **Baking sheets, lined with parchment paper**

1½ cups	all-purpose flour	375 mL
1 tsp	baking soda	5 mL
1 tsp	ground cinnamon	5 mL
1 cup	granulated sugar	250 mL
½ cup	firmly packed light brown sugar	125 mL
1 cup	butter, softened	250 mL
1	large egg	1
1 tsp	vanilla extract	5 mL
1½ cups	large-flake (old-fashioned) rolled oats	375 mL
1 cup	semisweet chocolate chips	250 mL

1. In a medium bowl, combine flour, baking soda and cinnamon.

2. In a large bowl, using an electric mixer on medium speed, beat granulated sugar, brown sugar and butter until light and creamy. Beat in egg and vanilla. With the mixer on low speed, beat in flour mixture until blended. Fold in oats and chocolate chips. Cover with plastic wrap and refrigerate for 1 hour, until chilled.

3. Preheat oven to 350°F (180°C).

4. Shape dough into 1-inch (2.5 cm) balls. Place 2 inches (5 cm) apart on prepared baking sheets.

5. Bake, one sheet at a time, for 10 to 12 minutes or until lightly browned around the edges. Let cool on pan on a wire rack for 5 minutes, then transfer to racks to cool completely.

Favorite Oatmeal Raisin Cookies

My father-in-law, an oatmeal cookie connoisseur, loves these cookies. He keeps begging me to make them again.

**MAKES
24 COOKIES**

Tips

Be sure to use large-flake (old-fashioned) rolled oats and not quick-cooking or instant oats.

Store cookies in an airtight container at room temperature for up to 1 week.

- Preheat oven to 350°F (180°C)
- Stand mixer
- Baking sheets, lined with parchment paper

½ cup	butter, softened	125 mL
1 cup	turbinado sugar	250 mL
1	large egg	1
2 tsp	vanilla extract	10 mL
1¼ cups	large-flake (old-fashioned) rolled oats	300 mL
⅔ cup	all-purpose flour	150 mL
1 tsp	baking powder	5 mL
½ tsp	baking soda	2 mL
½ tsp	salt	2 mL
½ tsp	ground cinnamon	2 mL
1 cup	golden raisins	250 mL

1. In stand mixer bowl, beat butter and sugar on medium-high speed until blended. Increase speed to high and beat for up to 2 minutes or until creamy. Reduce speed to medium and beat in egg and vanilla until combined.

2. Add oats, flour, baking powder, baking soda, salt and cinnamon. Beat on medium speed just until dough is completely blended. Fold in raisins.

3. Drop dough by tablespoonfuls (15 mL) about 2 inches (5 cm) apart on prepared baking sheets.

4. Bake, one sheet at a time, in preheated oven for 11 to 12 minutes or until the cookies are golden brown but slightly lighter in the center. Let cool on pan on a wire rack for 5 minutes, then transfer to racks to cool completely.

Trail Mix Cookies

Crumble these cookies for a healthy topping for your smoothie bowl, or enjoy them whole after a workout. They also are perfect to take along for a hike.

○○○

**MAKES
48 COOKIES**

Tips

If using larger dried fruit, chop them into smaller pieces before adding to the dough.

Be sure not to overbake these cookies, as they will continue to cook when you remove them from the oven. Remove them when they are lightly browned.

Store cookies in an airtight container at room temperature for up to 1 week.

- **Preheat oven to 350°F (180°C)**
- **Large baking sheets, lined with parchment paper**

1 cup	all-purpose flour	250 mL
½ tsp	baking soda	2 mL
¼ tsp	salt	1 mL
½ cup	light brown sugar	125 mL
⅓ cup	turbinado sugar	75 mL
¼ cup	butter, softened	60 mL
2	large egg whites	2
½ cup	liquid honey	125 mL
2 cups	large-flake (old-fashioned) rolled oats	500 mL
½ cup	green pumpkin seeds (pepitas)	125 mL
½ cup	unsalted sunflower seeds	125 mL
½ cup	mixed dried fruit (such as cranberries, cherries and blueberries)	125 mL
½ cup	mini semisweet chocolate chips	125 mL

1. In a medium bowl, combine flour, baking soda and salt.

2. In a large bowl, using an electric mixer on medium speed, beat brown sugar, turbinado sugar and butter until smooth. Beat in egg whites and honey. With the mixer on low speed, beat in flour mixture and oats until combined. Stir in pumpkin seeds, sunflower seeds, dried fruit and chocolate chips.

3. Drop dough by tablespoonfuls (15 mL) about 1 inch (2.5 cm) apart on prepared baking sheets.

4. Bake, one sheet at a time, in preheated oven for 8 to 10 minutes or until lightly browned. Let cool on pan on a wire rack for 5 minutes, then transfer to racks to cool completely.

Caramelized Bananas

Caramelized bananas make a delectably sweet topping for any dessert smoothie bowl. Spoon leftovers over yogurt, angel food cake or ice cream.

MAKES ABOUT 1 CUP (250 ML)

Tip

Peel and freeze overripe bananas in sealable plastic bags, to use in smoothie bowl recipes.

2 tbsp	butter	30 mL
2	ripe bananas, cut into ½-inch (1 cm) slices	2
2 tbsp	packed brown sugar	30 mL
½ tsp	ground cinnamon	2 mL

1. In a large skillet, melt butter over medium-low heat. Add bananas and brown sugar; cook, stirring gently, for about 5 minutes or until golden. Sprinkle with cinnamon.

Homemade Almond Butter

It's easy and economical to make your own fresh almond butter. All you need is almonds, salt and a food processor.

MAKES ABOUT ¾ CUP (175 ML)

Tips

Use a small food processor for this amount, or double or triple the recipe and use a medium or large food processor.

Try this recipe with raw almonds and toasted almonds to see which you like better.

• Food processor (see tip, at left)

1 cup	almonds	250 mL
Pinch	salt	Pinch

1. In food processor, pulse almonds and salt until crumbly, stopping occasionally to scrape down the sides. Process until thick and smooth.

2. Store in an airtight container in the refrigerator for up to 1 week.

Coconut Almond Butter

Use this nut butter in any smoothie bowl with chocolate and nuts, or try it as a spread on toast or graham crackers.

• **Food processor**

2 cups	almonds	500 mL
⅓ cup	unsweetened flaked coconut	75 mL
¼ tsp	salt	1 mL
1 tsp	virgin coconut oil	5 mL

1. In food processor, pulse almonds, coconut and salt until smooth, stopping occasionally to scrape down the sides. Add oil and process until creamy.

2. Store in an airtight container in the refrigerator for up to 1 week.

Variation

Use any of your favorite nuts in place of the almonds.

Cinnamon Cashew Nut Butter

These are some of my husband's favorite ingredients: cashews, honey and cinnamon. He loves this creamy nut butter stirred into smoothie bowls or just served with a spoon.

MAKES ABOUT ¾ CUP (175 ML)

Tip

To toast cashews, preheat the oven to 350°F (180°C). Spread nuts out in a single layer on a baking sheet lined with parchment paper. Bake for 10 to 15 minutes, stirring with tongs halfway through, until golden and fragrant. Immediately transfer to a bowl and let cool completely.

• **Food processor**

¾ cup	toasted cashews (see tip, at left)	75 mL
1 tsp	ground cinnamon	5 mL
⅛ tsp	salt	0.5 mL
2 tbsp	virgin coconut oil	30 mL
2 tbsp	liquid honey	30 mL

1. In food processor, pulse cashews, cinnamon, salt, coconut oil and honey until creamy, stopping occasionally to scrape down the sides.

2. Store in an airtight container in the refrigerator for up to 1 week.

Pecan Butter

Nut butters make smoothie bowl recipes more nutritious, more filling and thicker. Plus, they are packed with healthy fats and protein, so they keep you feeling full longer.

MAKES ABOUT 1¾ CUP (425 ML)

Tip

Toasting the pecans intensifies their flavor. You can also toast them in a preheated 350°F (180°C) oven, stirring occasionally, for 10 to 15 minutes, or until fragrant.

- **Food processor**

2 cups	pecan halves	500 mL
2 tsp	liquid honey	10 mL
Pinch	salt	Pinch
	Ground cinnamon (optional)	

1. In a large skillet, toast pecans over medium heat, stirring constantly, for about 4 minutes or until fragrant. Immediately transfer to a bowl and let cool completely.

2. In food processor, pulse pecans until finely chopped. Add honey, salt and cinnamon (if using) and process until creamy, stopping occasionally to scrape down the sides.

3. Store in an airtight container in the refrigerator for up to 1 week.

Pumpkin Walnut Butter

Pumpkin purée makes a fabulous addition to nut butter. My kids love this one stirred into smoothie bowls and oatmeal.

Tips

Use pumpkin purée, not pumpkin pie filling. The label should say "100% pure pumpkin."

You may substitute an equal amount of liquid honey for the maple syrup.

- **Preheat oven to 375°F (190°C)**
- **Food processor**

1 cup	walnut halves	250 mL
½ tsp	pumpkin pie spice	2 mL
¼ cup	pumpkin purée (not pie filling)	60 mL
1 tbsp	pure maple syrup	15 mL

1. Spread nuts in an even layer on a baking sheet. Roast in preheated oven for 6 to 8 minutes or until golden and fragrant. Immediately transfer to a bowl and let cool completely.

2. In food processor, pulse nuts until creamy, stopping occasionally to scrape down the sides. Add pumpkin pie spice, pumpkin purée and maple syrup; process until blended.

3. Store in an airtight container in the refrigerator for up to 1 week.

Variation

Substitute almonds or pecan halves for the walnuts.

Caramel Sauce

This mouthwatering sauce is a wonderful topping for dessert smoothie bowls.

MAKES ABOUT ¾ CUP (175 ML)

Tip

Store cooled caramel sauce in an airtight container in the refrigerator for up to 2 weeks.

¼ cup	butter	60 mL
1 cup	packed light brown sugar	250 mL
½ cup	milk	125 mL
Pinch	sea salt	Pinch
1 tbsp	vanilla extract	15 mL

1. In a medium saucepan, melt butter over medium-low heat. Whisk in brown sugar, milk and salt; cook, whisking gently, for about 7 minutes or until golden. Reduce heat to low and whisk in vanilla; cook for 1 to 2 minutes or until thickened. Serve warm or let cool.

Raspberry Sauce

This sauce is wonderful over the Banana Split (page 194) or any other smoothie bowl. Try it over ice cream, too!

MAKES ABOUT 3 CUPS (750 ML)

Tip

Store cooled raspberry sauce in an airtight container in the refrigerator for up to 1 week.

• **Blender or food processor**

2	packages (each 10 oz/300) frozen raspberries, thawed	2
¼ cup	granulated sugar	60 mL
1 tbsp	cornstarch	15 mL

1. In blender, purée raspberries. Press purée through a fine-mesh sieve into a bowl, discarding seeds.

2. In a medium saucepan, combine raspberry purée, sugar and cornstarch. Cook over low heat, stirring constantly, for 5 to 10 minutes or until thickened. Let cool completely. Serve cool or chilled.

Library and Archives Canada Cataloguing in Publication

Lewis, Alison, 1967–, author
  200 best smoothie bowl recipes / Alison Lewis.

Includes index.
ISBN 978-0-7788-0533-5 (paperback)

  1. Smoothies (Beverages). 2. One-dish meals. 3. Low-fat diet—Recipes. 4. Cookbooks.
I. Title. II. Title: Two hundred best smoothie bowl recipes.

TX817.S636L48 2016   641.87′5   C2015-908240-4

Index